MURDER & MAYHEM
— IN —
ULSTER COUNTY

A.J. SCHENKMAN & ELIZABETH WERLAU

Charleston · London

THE
History
PRESS

Published by The History Press
Charleston, SC 29403
www.historypress.net

First published 2013

Manufactured in the United States

ISBN 978.1.62619.073.3

Library of Congress CIP data applied for.

Notice: The information in this book is true and complete to the best of our knowledge. It is offered without guarantee on the part of the author or The History Press. The author and The History Press disclaim all liability in connection with the use of this book.

A.J. would like to dedicate this book, with love, to his son, Jonah.

Elizabeth would like to dedicate this book to Robert Werlau.

CONTENTS

Preface: "Ulcer County"   7
Acknowledgements   9

Part I: Murder
1. Ruined by Reading   13
2. The Curious Case of Charles W. Schmidle   18
3. The Ax That Felled Mr. Hasbrouck   21
4. The Merchant, the Maid…and a Murder?   26
5. Tramps, Berry Pickers and Slashings   31
6. Bad, Bad Willie Brown and the Monk Eastman Gang   38
7. I Think I May Have Hit Him   45
8. Boys Will Be Girls and Girls Will Be Boys   53

Part II: Mayhem
9. A Peaceful Mastication   61
10. Big Bad Bill Strikes Again   64
11. Hannah Markle's Saloon of Murder   74
12. Jailbreaks   80
13. Medicinal Purposes   87
14. Sleuthettes   91
15. Women's Work   95
16. A Cowboy in Old Ulster County   102
17. Occupational Hazards   109

Bibliography   117
About the Authors   127

Preface
"ULCER COUNTY"

If people wanted you to write warmly about them they should've behaved better.
—*Anne Lamott*

The *New York Herald* proclaimed in an 1870 edition of the paper that Ulster County, New York, was considered to be the "Ulcer County" of New York State. It quite pointedly wrote that this was due to its "lawlessness and crime." In the last "six months," the columnist wrote, "it has been the scene of no less than four cold blooded and brutal murders, six suicides and four elopements." It is prudent to say that this was quite an exaggeration, especially when compared to New York City's draft riots during the Civil War and locations such as the Five Points, which was much more dangerous than Ulster County in the 1870s.

Murder & Mayhem in Ulster County is the culmination of years of researching old newspapers and looking for scandalous headlines that piqued our interest and propelled both of us to investigate some of the villains of Ulster County's past. It must be put forth that as with *Wicked Ulster County*, a problem once again surfaced when working from newspapers in which there were inconsistencies in stories, dates and, in some cases, actual events. In many instances, other sources were used to confirm facts as much as possible. However, many of the stories in the newspapers were subject to interpretation by not only those who wrote them but also those who were interviewed. An example is the story about Victor Seydell. In one paper, his last name has one *l*; in others, his last name has two.

Though they most certainly have a historic significance, one must keep in mind that the stories contained in *Murder & Mayhem in Ulster County* are simply anecdotes discovered circulating in newspapers; in many cases, they have long since been forgotten. These are the tales of average citizens who lived out their lives in relative anonymity, with the exception of a few defining moments illustrated by the media. They were neither great individuals nor shapers of history; they were mostly ordinary people for whom, in some instances, the only testimonial that they even walked the earth are the newspaper articles we looked at over one hundred years after their lifetimes.

In closing, it is our hope that you take as much pleasure in reading this book as we did in writing it. We not only enjoyed the writing process but also relished visiting the locations where some of these crimes took place. Some of the sites of these events are vastly different than they were over one hundred years ago; thus, it took a lot of imagination to re-create events in our minds. However, in certain instances, the crime scenes are remarkably unchanged. In fact, where some of these heinous acts occurred, people go about their lives completely unaware that such tragic events transpired in their homes and on their properties.

Enjoy,
A.J. and Elizabeth

ACKNOWLEDGEMENTS

We would like to express gratitude to the many people who saw us through this book and to all those who provided support, talked things over, read, offered comments and assisted in the editing and proofreading. We would like to especially thank the following: Shirley Anson, the *Daily Freeman*, Ellenville Library and Museum, Glen Botto, the Gardiner Library, Michelle Greco, Ken Grey, Haviland-Heidgerd Collections, the Historical Society of Shawangunk and Gardiner, Historic Huguenot Street, Whitney Landis, Cory Mitchell, the Plattekill Historical Society and so many other people and places too numerous to list here. Last but not least, we want to give a heartfelt thanks to all of those in law enforcement who dedicated their time and risked their lives to serve justice to those individuals who provided us with the material for this book.

Part I
MURDER

1
RUINED BY READING

Around midnight on a cold winter's night in 1884, an unknown assailant entered the bedroom of Rondout saloon owner Edwin Kelland. He beat Kelland so severely that he was barely recognizable to his own brothers, who found him there the following afternoon. Kelland never regained consciousness after the attack, although according to sources, from time to time he raved incoherently and moved his hands about his face and head "as if warding off blows." The only possible motive for the assault of the popular business owner was robbery, for Kelland was known to sleep with the day's earnings from his billiards saloon at 44 John Street in a cigar box under his pillow each night. Along with the missing cigar box, thought to contain about seventy-five dollars in cash, authorities discovered that Kelland's distinctive silver watch and his sealskin cap were also gone.

Kelland died of his injuries two days later and was buried in Kingston's Wiltwyck Cemetery. He passed away without being able to identify his attacker; his testimony was little needed, however, as suspicion immediately fell on Charles Crosby, a young man of about seventeen or eighteen who had been employed by Kelland. Crosby, described as having "the usual inclination toward slovenliness," was seen leaving the city of Kingston wearing a smart outfit that included Kelland's black coat, green trousers and sealskin hat. Saloon patrons were able to supply authorities with some basic descriptions of Crosby's appearance, but it quickly became apparent that little else was known about the young man.

Crosby had been employed as a bartender by Kelland for about two months. Kelland, a member of several charitable organizations in the city of Kingston, had learned that the young man was homeless; thus, he allowed Crosby to sleep in the room next to his own and provided him with food and a job in the saloon. Normally, Crosby shared sleeping quarters with Kelland's brother Walter, but on the night of the attack, Walter was staying with a friend. Investigators noted that the flimsy wall separating the two bedrooms contained large cracks that would have made it easy for Crosby to see where Edwin Kelland hid his money each night.

It was determined that an assailant, using a large, brass beer faucet, had struck Kelland in the head hard enough to fracture his skull in two places. According to one report, a regular patron of the saloon noticed that the door to the pub was open the morning after the attack. He then entered the bar, and having discovered that no one was around, he made his way to Kelland's bedroom. The witness stated that he noticed Kelland was in bed and called out to him that the bar door was open, to which Kelland had supposedly replied, "Well, close it up then!" Aside from this report, no one else came forward to offer any information, other than the fact that the Kelland brothers had been talking for several days about the mysterious disappearance of the brass beer faucet.

Ulster County district attorney Alphonso T. Clearwater immediately authorized funds to search for Crosby in New York City and in the counties surrounding Ulster. The newspapers were quick to find Crosby guilty, with headlines describing the teenager as a "Boy Murderer" and "A Youth Who Has Been Ruined by Dime Novel Reading." The story took a strange turn just days later when the Ulster County sheriff discovered that there was not just one but two young men by the name of Charles Crosby in Ulster County—neither of them the man they had been looking for. The Crosby cousins, as they were known, lived in the town of Marlborough near the border of the town of Plattekill. While these gentlemen were not whom the authorities had been seeking, they felt they knew exactly who had committed the murder of Edwin Kelland: Massachusetts native Louis Willett.

The Crosby cousins explained that they had first met Willett when he arrived in Marlborough looking for work during the previous summer. He had shown up with a group of other men who were in search of employment as berry pickers on one of the Hudson Valley's many farms. The Poughkeepsie Transportation Company would drop off hundreds of young men each year in a similar manner, and farmers would have their pick of hired hands to help bring in their crops.

$1,000 REWARD!

ULSTER'S DISTRICT ATTORNEY'S OFFICE,
KINGSTON, N. Y., January 18th, 1884.

The Board of Supervisors of the County of Ulster offer a reward of $1,000 to any person who will arrest and surrender to the Sheriff of Ulster County the murderer of Edwin Kelland, who is supposed to be LOUIS WILLETTE *alias* CHARLES CROSBY.

The crime was committed at Kingston on the 8th day of January, 1884.

Willette is of French descent, about 18 years old, 5 feet 8 inches high, dark complexion, very black eyes, straight black hair, slightly round-shouldered, of boyish appearance; is inclined to be slovenly; is a good Pool player; has been a cotton spinner, a boatman and a berry picker; has a decided taste for flash reading, he wore when he left Kingston a black diagonal sack coat the sleeves of which were too short for him, greenish colored trousers, buttoned shoes with faded green cloth tops; he carried a double case silver watch with gold-plated chain to which was attached as a charm a five cent nickel without the word "cents."

To avoid disputes the certificate of the District Attorney of Ulster County is made final and conclusive evidence of the right of the person presenting it to such reward.

A requisition upon the Governor of any State in the Union with the warrant of the Governor of the State of New York will be furnished by the subscriber on his being furnished with reasonable proof that Willette has been apprehended.

Information regarded as important may be sent by telegraph to the subscriber, who will pay for the transmission of the message.

A. T. CLEARWATER,
District Attorney of Ulster County, Kingston, N. Y.

An example of a reward postcard sent from the Ulster County District Attorney's Office offering a reward for the capture of Edwin Kelland. *Elizabeth Werlau's collection.*

Willett found work on the Marlborough farm of Patrick Barry. Barry would later report that Willett preferred to read trashy newspapers and five-cent novels to working and was soon fired following an incident in which he arrived at work intoxicated and enraged. Barry also said that upon leaving, Willet claimed that when he eventually returned home to Massachusetts, his former employer "could just bet his life he would have a nobby suit of clothes, a gold watch and chain, and considerable 'chink.'"

Following the incident at Barry's, Willett found work on the nearby farm of Eli Harcourt. Harcourt described the boy as being a strong worker but also as someone with an unhealthy fascination with crime novels and "flash literature." Harcourt would later tell a reporter that the boy's "whole frame would be in a tremor of excitement and his eyes glisten[ing] while holding one of the Jesse James series in his hand." Willett met the Crosby cousins while boarding with the Sidney Barnhart family, who lived near the Harcourt farm. He shared his love of criminal stories with the young boys and invited them to take part in his next adventure.

With the first Charles, son of William Crosby, Willett exchanged clothing and satchels. He then convinced the other Charles, son of yet another Charles Crosby, to run away with him and seek employment driving mules for the Delaware and Hudson Canal. The second Charles soon returned home to Marlborough while Willett made his way to Kingston. With borrowed clothes and an appropriated name, Willett began working for Kelland under the alias of "Charles Crosby."

Willett traveled through several states but was drawn back to Ulster County in May 1884, presumably to learn how the search for Kelland's attacker was going. Working under yet another alias, he took a job on the Dayton Fruit Farm in the town of Marlborough, about twenty miles away from the scene of the crime. A young boy recognized Willett, who in turn offered him $10 to keep silent. The boy told only his father, who immediately contacted Marlborough Constable Mackey in hopes of receiving the $1,000 reward advertised for Willett's capture.

By the time Mackey reached Dayton's farm, Willett was on the run once again. A search of the train cars and the steamboats coming in and out of Milton over the next few days proved fruitless because Willett had sneaked back to Dayton's under the cover of darkness one night. Once there, he stole three dollars and all of the worldly possessions of "an Italian woman in the picker's quarters." With his newfound wealth, Willett set out for Newburgh, where he was able to secure passage to New York City. From the city, Willett would make occasional trips back to Ulster County to check on the progress of his case. In late June of that year, he was seen drinking beer at a Milton bar and working once again for Dayton.

Willett was eventually arrested in New York City in early July, after he was witnessed loitering around liquor stores day after day. A reporter from the *New York Times* located a diary in one of the rooms Willett had been renting, written in the style of the novels the teenager so adored. Though penned by a young man, the diary entries depicted the thought process of a coldblooded killer, "who considered he would be safer from detection in Ulster County than anywhere else."

On July 3, 1884, Willett was brought by train to Rhinebeck in Dutchess County. District Attorney Alphonso T. Clearwater wanted to avoid the publicity that would surely be generated if Willett were brought to the ferryboat landing in Kingston. Instead, he arranged to have Willett ferried from Rhinebeck to the dock of the steamship *Mary Powell*. Clearwater's instincts proved correct, for nearly two thousand people gathered in vain at the ferry landing to catch a glimpse of the alleged murderer while Willett arrived at the Ulster County Jail in Kingston with little notice.

The New York State Supreme Court case of the people, respondents, versus Louis Willett, appellate, went to trial late that fall. Willett, represented by attorney William Lounsberry, claimed self-defense and stated that when he entered Kelland's bedroom area, Kelland called out to him and accused him of stealing seventy-five cents from a pair of pants hanging in the room. Willett explained that Kelland hit him, forcing him to run from the room and grab the beer faucet in order to strike Kelland to defend himself. He maintained that he fled in fear, taking Kelland's money and clothing without thinking. However, Clearwater implored the jury to consider the premeditation of the crime in light of the fact that the beer faucet had been missing for days.

After deliberating for four hours, the jury found Willett guilty of murder in the first degree. Judge Peckham delivered a sentence that had not been heard of in Ulster County for nearly eighty years: Willett was sentenced "to be hanged January 22, 1885, in the County Jail, between 8 A.M. and 2 P.M." The eighteen-year-old Willett "flushed slightly, but otherwise took matters coolly."

Appeals were made, and as a result, the case was tried again later in 1885. These actions only delayed the inevitable, as the original sentence held. The May 21, 1886 Friday afternoon edition of the *Troy Daily Times* described Willett's final morning:

> *At 9:15 o'clock this morning Louis Willett alias Crosby suffered the extreme penalty of the law in the Ulster County Jail at Kingston for the murder of Edwin Kelland on the evening of January 7, 1884 in this city. He died easily. Willett passed his last hours on earth in a cell the window of which is directly opposite the building in which the murder was deliberately planned and coolly perpetrated in cold blood.*

The reporter went on to describe Willett's "comfortable" final hours, which included religious services in his Ulster County Jail cell given by several members of the local clergy and a breakfast of "beefsteak, fried eggs, fried potatoes and a cup of coffee," which he declined. Willett refused to speak any last words and snubbed a request to confess, remaining "cool and collected when the death warrant was read to him, not a muscle of his face moving." At 9:10 a.m., the condemned man was walked to the gallows at the jail, where he put his hands behind his back to be tied together without having to be asked. The rope was drawn up, and Willett's neck broke; his heart stopped beating four minutes later. This thus ended the life of the teenager who had lived out his fantasy of committing a crime worthy of the "blood and thunder novels of the five cent order" that had held such sway over him.

2

THE CURIOUS CASE OF
CHARLES W. SCHMIDLE

In the early hours of November 25, 1907, Charles W. Schneider made his way from the Benning Racetrack, where he had earlier cheered for horses from a vast grandstand, to Lafayette Square. Lafayette Square had been in existence for only a little over one hundred years. The National Park Service states that the park had once been part of the White House grounds, and presidents enjoyed its desired gardens. This changed after Thomas Jefferson became president, as he carved the area out of the White House grounds and created what would become Pennsylvania Avenue.

In 1907, President Theodore Roosevelt occupied the White House. During this time, Schneider sat down on one of the benches in Lafayette Square, near a home once owned by Dolly Madison. He slowly raised a pistol to his temple and pulled the trigger once. This action set up a mystery that would end in a little eastern Ulster County hamlet known as Clintondale.

November 25 was a Monday; thus, many people slowly made their way out of their homes to work. Others took a stroll through the park. Several of these people saw a man lying facedown in the grass of Lafayette Square with a bullet lodged in his brain. The pistol that lay next to his hand was still warm. As the man still had a faint pulse, the police were called, along with an ambulance.

Once an ambulance arrived, a curious turn of events was set into motion. Those handling the body of the man found in the park relayed to reporters that it was the body of a Charles W. Schneider of Clintondale, New York. The ambulance rushed Schneider to the local hospital, where he eventually died of his wound. Doctors recognized immediately that this death was not

Lafayette Park from the White House in Washington, D.C. This is the way Schmidle might have seen it on that fateful day. *Courtesy of the Library of Congress.*

the result of a murder; they surmised that Schneider had most likely died due to a self-inflicted gunshot wound to his head. The police and hospital staff started thoroughly searching through the deceased man's clothing for information so that they could notify his next of kin of what happened. They did not realize that they had made a dreadful mistake in identifying the lifeless body before them; it was not Schneider.

On November 12, 1907, a roughly sixty-year-old C.W. Schmidle had left his home in Clintondale, New York. He lived there with his wife, Marguerite, and his stepdaughter on a small, thirteen-acre fruit farm. This was one of many fruit farms in the area. In 1904, Schmidle had purchased the farm from Ward D. Gunn after moving to Clintondale from Brooklyn in New York City. He still owned the home he had lived in before moving upstate.

Schmidle's destination was the Brooklyn Trust Company; he was going to pay over $200 in taxes he owed on Number 178 South Elliott Place in the Fort Greene section of Brooklyn. This area contained mostly "single-family brownstones dating to the 1860s." Today, it is famous for being home to the offices of celebrities such as Spike Lee.

Investigators were able to piece together that Schmidle never ended up in Brooklyn but instead traveled to Washington, D.C., where he eventually made his way to the Benning Racetrack. A "grand stand coupon for the track" was later found in one of his pockets by investigators. According to the website entitled "Lost Washington, D.C.," Congress eventually put a stop to betting at the Benning Racetrack because of "shady betting practices." When in operation, it was a destination not only for congressmen but also for many in the Northeast. In fact, during the same year that Congress ended betting at the track, advertisements for the start of the season still ran in local papers. This all happened about a year too late to save Schmidle.

The pockets of the deceased Schmidle were searched; his personal effects revealed where he lived and also listed his wife and a sister named "Mrs. Michaelis." While the possibility of a murder was initially investigated, it became apparent that Schmidle took his own life after he lost money at the track that he was going to use to pay off the balance of taxes he owed on his home in Brooklyn. The fact that he had only fifty-four cents in his pocket lent credence to the theory that he had squandered his money.

Schneider was eventually identified as Schmidle not by investigators but rather by his neighbors. When word began to filter back that a Schneider of Clintondale had committed suicide in a park in Washington, D.C., the citizens of Clintondale did not consider the news for long because they knew that no one by that name lived in their small hamlet. Once all the personal information of the departed man was known, however, the facts were put together, and it was realized that it was not Schneider but in fact Schmidle who had killed himself. The *Daily Freeman* boasted that it had broken the case, though in the process, at least one reporter unknowingly committed the same type of error that the first authorities on the scene did—in some editions spelled the name as C.M. Schmiddle.

3
THE AX THAT FELLED MR. HASBROUCK

Levi Bodine spent most of his life with Daniel A. Hasbrouck. He was brought from the county poorhouse on Libertyville Road just outside New Paltz, where he was born, to Hasbrouck's home in Ohioville located on the Lloyd–New Paltz border. Bodine was the son of Aletta Ann Bodine, who went on to have six more children. Like one of his other siblings, Bodine was born deaf. Perhaps to give Bodine a better chance at life, his mother agreed to allow the wealthy Hasbrouck to take him into his family. It was hoped by his mother that Bodine would be able to learn some sort of trade.

Hasbrouck was about forty years old in 1870. He had been married to Sarah L. VanOrden in 1858, until her death in 1868. The couple had one child, whom they named Elizabeth. In 1870, Hasbrouck remarried and took his late wife's sister, Elsie, as his bride. The couple had a young child, who was born during the prior winter, in February 1869.

Hasbrouck was a prosperous man who had a large farm; it was actually one of the biggest in the area, so he could afford to have others work for him. According to the 1860 federal census, Hasbrouck was wealthy enough to have two servants. One of the servants is listed in the census as an African American man named Levi Hasbrouck; the surname of Bodine does not appear. He was ten years old. It is believed that Bodine actually lived in the tenant house that Hasbrouck had built for his farmhands.

Bodine did much of the manual labor on Hasbrouck's farm. Frequently, Hasbrouck instructed Bodine to chop wood and then stack it. According to Bodine, Hasbrouck could be abusive toward him at times; he complained to others about this through his limited use of sign language. If there had been friction between Hasbrouck and Bodine, no one could pinpoint exactly when it started, as later court testimony would reveal. Bodine claimed that Hasbrouck whipped him for the slightest infraction or if he did not complete a task to Hasbrouck's satisfaction. Hasbrouck seemed unaware of the growing discord between Bodine and himself. As would be divulged in court, some farmhands knew that sooner or later the situation between Bodine and Hasbrouck was going to end badly.

Hasbrouck's friends and family worried about him. They were mostly concerned about the young man he had adopted from the county poorhouse, as he had threatened to kill Hasbrouck on several occasions. Bodine had signed his plans to some of the other farmhands; however, they often were able to talk him out of pursuing his intentions. Hasbrouck was well aware of the threats made against his life, though he did not appear to take them seriously.

On February 15, 1870, a cold morning, Hasbrouck surveyed his dwindling wood supply and instructed Bodine to approach the woodpile and start splitting wood. Bodine did what he was told, without incident, and chopped lumber until late in the morning when Hasbrouck appeared. According to later newspaper reports, Hasbrouck signed for Bodine to "yoke the oxen" in order to load the wood. Bodine did not move fast enough and was met with Hasbrouck's hand. Bodine exploded in anger and repeatedly swung his ax at Hasbrouck, until he had struck him several times. As Bodine attempted his seventh blow, Hasbrouck managed to grab the ax; the two men struggled for the weapon, but Bodine was much stronger than his master and prevailed in holding on to it. Hasbrouck wrestled free of Bodine and bolted for his house. When he was within steps of his home, he tripped. Bodine quickly appeared and dropped the ax twice into the back of the fallen man's head.

Albert Conklin and Luther Lefever, who were in Hasbrouck's main house, heard a commotion outside and ran to the window just in time to see Bodine sink his ax into Hasbrouck's skull. Bodine, covered in blood, looked up to see Conklin and Lefever coming toward him; he dropped his ax and fled to what he thought was the safety of his tenant house. The two men pursued him into his residence, where they discovered a crying Bodine. They grabbed him and tied him up tightly with rope to secure him until authorities could arrive and take custody of him. Meanwhile, more people who noticed the disturbances began emptying out of the main house. Some individuals attended to Hasbrouck, who was lying on the ground unconscious with blood pouring from his wounds. A doctor was summoned, but when he arrived he proclaimed that the ax had done too much damage and that Hasbrouck had lost too much blood. Shortly after the doctor appeared, Hasbrouck perished.

By the time a sheriff came onto the scene, the news of Hasbrouck's death had already spread like wildfire and had reached New Paltz. As the sheriff entered a New Paltz jail with Bodine, a large angry mob was waiting. They demanded that the sheriff hand over Bodine to them so that they could administer justice faster than any judge or jury. Similarly, according to the *New York Herald*, the police officer who escorted the alleged killer of Hasbrouck admitted that he tried to give Bodine chances to escape, as it would have been his pleasure to shoot down the "killer." The sheriff felt that it would be best for Bodine's safety if he brought him to the Ulster County Jail in Kingston.

Bodine made it alive to the Ulster County Jail and awaited what he was sure would be a sentence of death by hanging. To illustrate this, he made a gesture of a rope being tied around his neck with his eyes rolling to the top of his head. He cried an almost constant stream of tears thinking about the fate before him.

A reporter traveled from New York City to Kingston, where he interviewed, with an interpreter, the alleged killer of Hasbrouck. Bodine made it clear that he was provoked and that he would not have swung at Hasbrouck for no reason. He indicated that Hasbrouck was the aggressor and that he was only defending himself. Bodine re-created the events before the killing, placing his two hands around his own throat to illustrate how Hasbrouck had been choking him prior to his attack. He reiterated that he had to protect himself because he feared that Hasbrouck was going to murder him.

Bodine continued that his guardian regularly beat and whipped him. His accusations against Hasbrouck would be countered by a litany of witnesses, who all asserted that they had either viewed the slaying or heard Bodine, on numerous occasions, make threats against Hasbrouck. Michael Hays, a farmhand, testified that during the very same morning in which Bodine killed Hasbrouck, he had confessed his plans to eliminate him. Hays attested that he had advised Bodine not to commit such a lethal act. Some other witnesses painted a portrait of Bodine as a violent and disturbed individual. For example, it was recounted that he frequently tortured animals, having a particular hatred of cats.

By October 1870, a trial was underway. It was presided over by Judge Hogeboom. The Ulster County district attorney at the time, Westbrook,

One of the insane asylums where Levi Bodine stayed after the killing.
Courtesy of the Library of Congress.

needed to prove that Bodine was able to recognize the charges against him. The judge already refused to accept a plea by Bodine, unless it could be proven that he understood what would be happening to him. Westbrook argued before a jury that Bodine was sane and that he could not only speak but also had the ability to hear loud noises. He explained that "neighbors and family of the deceased were able to communicate with the prisoner by sign and make themselves understood." On the other hand, defense lawyer D.M. DeWitt countered the prosecution with an insanity defense. He explained to the courtroom that the man before them was uneducated, deaf, dumb and mute. He continued that Bodine was unable to converse with him in any way, and he was thus incapable of articulating the charges or proceedings against him.

Even experts disagreed with regard to Bodine's level of understanding. Dr. Wirt, a physician, felt that Bodine could comprehend and correspond with people. Alternately, Dr. Isaac L. Peet, a principal at a school for deaf students, felt that Bodine could not grasp all that was occurring around him. Another expert witness, who was "deaf and mute," concurred with Peet. A newspaper reporter found it shocking that at one point, the court suggested that Bodine be educated at Peet's school with the intention of hanging him at a future date. This idea was rejected, especially by Peet. Peet did proclaim, however, that he would take custody of Bodine for the purpose of education only.

Bodine's trial created quite a quandary for Ulster County's judicial system, especially since newspapers started keeping tallies on how expensive the process was becoming for the taxpayers of the county. The trial continued into 1871, with little headway made. Finally, in January 1871, the jury reported to the judge four times that it could

not reach a unanimous decision about the sanity of Bodine. Eventually, Bodine was judged to be insane and was committed to the Auburn Hospital for the Insane. He was later transferred to the Matteawan State Hospital for the Insane.

The story of Bodine came to an end in November 1914, when, after forty-two years of being incarcerated, he had tired of his situation. There was an ice pond on the grounds of the state hospital where he resided. When no one was watching him, Bodine made his way out to the pond. He leapt in and drowned himself. His body was later found by staff—he was sixty-five years old.

4

THE MERCHANT, THE MAID...
AND A MURDER?

Annie Hommell of Saugerties was born into a poor German family and entered into service as a young girl to help ease the financial difficulties of her parents. Throughout her teenage years, young Hommell seemed to be living a life far more prosperous than the one she had left behind. She wore beautifully designed clothing that belied her status as a maid and was known in the village for her beauty. Her seemingly good fortune ended, however, at the age of twenty when the unmarried and noticeably pregnant young woman disappeared from her Ulster County home.

Hommell was employed at the age of thirteen or fourteen by Moses Schoenfeld, a Prussian native and veteran of the Civil War described in the papers of the time as a stout man in his midforties who was "a wealthy merchant tailor, a well-to-do-Jew, who has a fine house." The striking young woman worked for Schoenfeld and his wife for about seven years. By early 1877, Schoenfeld's wife began spending extensive periods of time in New York City for treatment of an unknown illness. At the same time, Hommell began seeing several Saugerties-area physicians for a case of dropsy, although none could determine a remedy to ease the condition.

Reports from the village described an open relationship developing between Schoenfeld and his maid upon his wife's absence, and some reported seeing him kissing Hommell in public. By the end of that year, Hommell was thought to be pregnant, and on December 15, 1877, she went missing from her home in the village. She had announced to her parents that she was leaving to seek a remedy for her illness in either New York

Tivoli Station, where Annie Hommell allegedly met a mysterious woman on a train bound for New York City. *Elizabeth Werlau's collection.*

City or Philadelphia, but she offered little other information. Some residents reported that Hommell took a ferry to Tivoli, where she boarded a train for New York City; others recounted seeing her meet an older woman at the train station who claimed to be a doctor's wife.

At that point, the story took several wild turns. Some reports indicate that Hommell met a woman on the train who may have been employed by the Schoenfelds to become a sort of guardian for the young woman. Schoenfeld disappeared within days of Hommell and, upon his later return to Saugerties, began regularly making trips to New York City.

Within a few days of Hommell's disappearance, letters began arriving for both Schoenfeld and George Hommell, Annie's father. The first letters were signed in her name but appeared to be written in a man's handwriting while later letters were simply signed by "M.D." The postmarks on the letters and contents within them suggested that Hommell was moving to various addresses in Brooklyn and Philadelphia. The letters sent to Hommell's parents each month contained the sum of five dollars.

Hommell's father was becoming increasingly more convinced that Schoenfeld knew of her whereabouts and thus began speaking harshly of him around Saugerties. In an effort to clear his name, Schoenfeld accompanied the man on a trip to Brooklyn to seek out his daughter's whereabouts; he also offered reward money to whoever could provide additional information. Unfortunately, the trip proved fruitless.

The ferry at Saugerties, where some Saugerties residents reported seeing Annie Hommell travel to Tivoli to catch a train. *Elizabeth Werlau's collection.*

According to the *New York Times,* Mr. and Mrs. Hommell received a final letter from M.D. postmarked August 19, 1878, from Philadelphia, Pennsylvania. The simple note bore devastating news for the family:

> *Dearest Mrs. Hommel* [sic]: *It is hard for me that I could not before, but now as it is possible for me to do so, I think it is my duty to inform you of your daughter. She has suffered much in the bowels, and the blood became water, as in the case of all dropsical cases. She suffered also from cramps and became insensible, so that I could not obtain her address, but now, when the woman who attended your daughter came back from the country, I learned your address and now I must communicate to you the fact that your beloved daughter has, spite of all my medical help, gone to the better home. Her last words were "Dear Mother, don't forget your Annie." Respectfully your friend, M.D.*

The payments to Hommell's parents ceased with this letter, as did any further contact from the mysterious M.D. Written communications with Hommell's sister, Mary, who lived in Philadelphia, indicated that they had no interaction with each other after December 1877. Furthermore, she believed her sister to be dead as a result of foul play. For a short time, at Mrs. Schoenfeld's request, Hommell's sister returned to Saugerties to live with the Schoenfelds and later wrote to her father: "I am often sorry I went to live there after Annie left. I am sorry I didn't heed what people said. I have found out now what the talk of people amounts to."

In the meantime, Schoenfeld was charged in connection with Hommell's disappearance, but he was not arrested. Prominent citizens of Saugerties, including attorney Peter Cantine and Reverend Philip Lichtenberg of the German Lutheran Church of Saugerties, became involved in the investigation and helped garner community support against Schoenfeld. Schoenfeld responded by making even more frequent trips to the city, purportedly for the purpose of searching for clues.

Shortly after receiving the final letter from M.D., the Hommell family heard news of a grisly discovery made in a Staten Island graveyard. Three young boys herding cattle near the Silver Lake Cemetery, a Jewish burial ground, came upon a barrel partially buried on the property. Upon further examination, it was discovered that the barrel contained the decomposing body of a woman. After a month without any clues as to her identity, the body was reinterred in a nearby potter's field. News of the body eventually reached Saugerties, where Hommell's family was still holding out hope that she would be found alive.

Hommell was described by her parents as "being of medium size, good figure and having dark brown hair, and good teeth"; the body found in the cemetery matched this description. Comparisons of hair and a missing back tooth further supported the claim that this might be the corpse of Hommell. Hommell's father traveled to New York City with Cantine and Lichtenberg to further assist in her identification. The body was exhumed from the potter's field and was recognized as Hommell by her father and Lichtenberg on the basis of its hair and teeth. Lichtenberg was quoted as saying that he saw Hommell on a daily basis and was "positive it was Annie's hair." The clothing on the woman, however, could not be definitively matched to any item that she had owned.

A day later, Schoenfeld and his wife, along with their attorney, Carroll Whitaker, also traveled to Staten Island to help in the identification of Hommell. Upon examining the body, Schoenfeld and his wife asserted that the woman could not be Hommell, as her hair was too short to match that of their maid's—she had never cut her hair in the time she was employed by the couple.

The body was once again buried, but on Cantine's later insistence, doctors involved in the case made the decision to unearth it for a second time to determine whether a match could be made based on a fractured wrist Hommell had suffered as a teen. In order to make the determination, they cut the arms at the shoulders from the figure and employed "an insane pauper" to boil them in order to remove the decomposing flesh and check the bones beneath. Once this was done, they determined that the arms had never been fractured and that the skeleton most likely belonged to a woman in her later thirties.

After investigating the cases of several missing women in the New York City area, the body was eventually determined to be that of Mary Ann Degnan of Staten Island. Her husband, Edward Reinhardt, was identified by a witness as the person who had originally buried the barrel containing Degnan. He was later convicted of killing his wife in order to marry his second wife.

With the body positively identified, the last traces of Hommell vanished. The local newspapers continued to follow the case for several years, but few leads were ever discovered. Schoenfeld's business prospered, and from time to time the local papers would offer commentary on the existence of "the evil man" who continued to operate in the community where he had been at the center of so much scandal. Eventually, those types of articles gave way to others praising Schoenfeld for remaining active in the search for Hommell when even family members had given up all hope.

By the time he passed away in 1914, Schoenfeld's alleged role in Annie Hommell's disappearance had all but been forgotten. The newspapers that had once condemned him as a criminal only praised his success in business and the work ethic that kept him directly involved with his many stores right up until a few years before his death.

5

TRAMPS, BERRY PICKERS AND SLASHINGS

Emma Brooks kept to herself and preferred to live alone in her home in Highland, New York, located just outside New Paltz. Other people though, such as her neighbors, recalled that it was not always that way. She had once loved a local Episcopal minister; however, this had been long ago and the courtship never reached marriage. The neighborhood gossips spoke of a woman who never wedded because she never stopped loving this man.

These same chatterers also remembered the big house that she once shared with her father, Joshua Brooks, "a well-to-do fruit grower in Ulster County." When he died, he left the orchard and house to his daughter. When the home burned sometime later, she moved into a smaller house and only interacted with those around her when it was related to business. No one ever accused her of being rude or inhospitable, just professional in her interactions with people. Her exception to this rule was Lorenzo Bragg, or "Reny," as she called him. In 1909, he was reportedly in his forties, and he managed her daily affairs. He had come to live with Brooks as a ten-year-old boy.

Just as some fruit growers do today, Brooks used to hire seasonal workers to help her haul in fruit to be sold at the local market. A particularly labor-intensive enterprise was the picking of berries, especially the currants she grew. The people she hired were mostly from the local community, such as Constable Alfred Williams, yet others were transient individuals. Some laborers would stay the season, while others would pick produce for a day or two to earn some money for alcohol or to get to their next destination. Many felt that some of these "tramps" were quite unsavory characters, especially John Babbitt, who was also known as John Cooley.

Cooley was quite an interesting character. He was a "drunkard who proclaimed to anyone his love of the bottle" and who worked solely to get himself to the next drink. He was about forty years old with a dark complexion and weighed between 150 and 160 pounds. The almost six-foot-tall Cooley wore a dark shirt with the left sleeve torn down from the shoulder and a black derby: "In another time someone might even call him handsome."

Something about Cooley did not sit right with those who encountered him, especially Brooks. She remarked more than a few times that she could not wait to rid herself of this "tramp" berry picker. He began making it a habit of peering into and milling about her home. He also questioned Brooks about money.

Typically, Cooley would collect his wages, go to the local tavern and then reappear at Brooks's place for more work. During the week of July 9, 1909, he conducted the usual "collecting his seventy cents in wages," and according to a local paper, he announced his intention of "drinking till he could not stand anymore" at a nearby pub. About a week later, he again approached Brooks to obtain additional work; he was told that he was no longer needed and to go away. However, Cooley did not depart. Instead, he started following the old woman around her property and annoying her in attempts to solicit work from her.

Constable Williams earned extra money by picking berries for Brooks. Sometimes after collecting his pay and dropping off a box of currants to her house, the two would briefly talk. On the morning of July 14, 1909, he noticed Cooley loitering around Brooks's home. It was obvious that he was causing the old woman to become flustered.

After Williams identified himself, he instructed Cooley to move on and to quit being a nuisance to Brooks. Cooley appeared to acquiesce—eyewitnesses later remembered that he left the property in the early afternoon of July 14, 1909. Then, a motorman for the New Paltz–Highland Trolley recalled that Cooley returned to Brooks's farm later that same afternoon, at about 5:00 p.m. He also recounted ejecting him for "refusing to pay his fare."

Before Cooley returned to Brooks's home, he went to the house of her neighbor, Mary Ellen Townsend. When Townsend inquired what the man wanted, he asked if he could buy some buttermilk. While she fetched the goods, he presumably started asking questions about Brooks.

After the vagrant received his buttermilk, he made his way back to Brooks's home, where he found Brooks and Williams sitting on the porch and chatting.

Cooley decided to join them. At one point, the constable overheard Cooley asking Brooks where she kept her money and if she held on to it herself or gave it to Bragg. The constable ran Cooley off the property, along with some other men who had joined him and were now waiting in the front of the house. Cooley did not stay away long.

Bragg grew up in Brooks's house and assisted her with the farm. He performed odd jobs and supervised the day-to-day operations of the land, especially during the berry-picking season. Although Brooks had relatives in the area, she treated Bragg as part of her family, as he was the closest thing to a son she would ever have. In fact, in 1907 she planned to deed her house and fruit farm to him when she died. Therefore, Bragg did not collect wages from Brooks, as he felt that her possessions would become his soon enough.

At times, Bragg's surrogate mother would try to discuss financial matters with him, even sharing that she kept money on her person at all times. He quickly remarked that he did not want to know anything about her capital, including where she retained it or how much she had. This way, if something were to happen, he could truly say that he knew nothing about Brooks's funds, especially since he had noticed the inquisitive Cooley slithering about the house and farm—he did not have a good feeling about this man.

Another person who felt uncomfortable about Cooley was Townsend. On the same day that Cooley had been harassing Brooks, July 14, 1909, Townsend paid a visit to her. Some accounts state that she was delivering some buttermilk, while others assert that she was collecting wages for picking berries. As the two women talked on Brooks's porch, the tramp Cooley came skulking around again. Brooks agreed with Townsend about distrusting him, and she hesitated to take out money in front of him because he was always trying to see how much she had.

When it came time to pay Townsend, Brooks asked the woman to go inside the house with her. Once there, she produced two small pocketbooks that had been sewn into pockets underneath her dress. One pocketbook contained $300; the other contained less than $20. After receiving her wages, Townsend left Brooks's home; she would be the last person to see her alive.

Sometime about 6:00 p.m., Bragg realized that he had not encountered Cooley or Brooks in some time. He approached Brooks's house and called to her; there was no answer. Bragg opened her back door and proceeded slowly to the front of the house. He gasped as he saw Brooks lying on the floor in a pool of blood. He ran to her side and saw that her throat had been cut from ear to ear. The only thing holding her head to her body was her spinal column. In addition, lying next to Brooks were two empty pocketbooks that had been torn from her dress; immediately, Cooley's face flashed through his mind.

Bragg rushed to an automobile and drove to Coroner Hasbrouck's to alert him to what had happened. Hasbrouck, in turn, notified Doctor Blakeley, and the three went back to Brooks's house. Brooks's body was examined by both men and was transported to a local funeral parlor for a later autopsy. The authorities were then alerted. The first two men on the scene were Ulster County sheriff Boice and Dutchess County undersheriff Manning Cleveland. Cleveland brought along his well-known bloodhounds to sniff for clues.

An initial search of Brooks's property turned up the weapon that was used to kill her. It had been discarded under her house with her blood still on it. The bloodhounds had also found a scent and followed it to Chestnut Grove near a stream where discarded clothing was found stained with blood. Also, a pencil that was identified by Braggs as the one Brooks wore in her hair was later found by the stream. Many different footprints were discovered, leading the officers to believe that more than one person was involved in the murder. The bloodhounds continued to track a smell all the way out to the railroad, which ran near the front of the house; they then lost the trail.

Wanted posters were distributed containing a description of the assailant, as well as a reward offer for his capture. Considering the $200 reward, it did not take long for arrests to be made. An individual supposedly matching the portrayal of Cooley was arrested in Dutchess County; he was later released on July 20, 1909.

William Foth, also referred to as a tramp, was arrested in late July. Authorities did not believe that he had committed the Brooks crime, but they did feel that he had access to information that could lead to two other men who did commit the crime. In addition to Cooley, the lawmen were also searching for a Jan Kubaly.

Residents of Highland reported that it was believed that Foth was given some kind of payoff, as he held a large sum of money shortly after Brooks's death. Foth admitted to being at the scene of the crime and even confessed to riding a trolley with Cooley. After being questioned by authorities, Foth was brought to the Ulster County Jail.

A more promising lead appeared at the Prattsville Hotel in Greene County, where an alert hotel employee noticed a man fitting the description of Cooley undressing in a barn. He was observed changing out of clothing that matched the description of Cooley's garb on the wanted posters. According to testimony, this man informed guests at the hotel that he was a berry picker

The billy club, a police officer's best friend in some cases for intimidation. One smack with this piece of hardwood might make you think twice. *Courtesy of the Library of Congress.*

and that he had made his way there from Highland. This convinced these people further that the man standing before them was the one wanted by Sheriff Boice. By the time the Sheriff's Office was notified of this interloper, he had already moved on to an unknown location.

Despite his disappearance from the hotel, this curious person was later picked up by the police. It turns out that he was not Cooley, but another man named Dennis O'Brien. He was quite a bit taller than Cooley and heavier as well. O'Brien had come to Prattsville looking for work, but when he saw that there was little available, he headed back to Connecticut, where he claimed to be from. He appeared angry at one point, as he desired to be arrested so that he would have a nice, warm place to sleep. Instead, he claimed that the sheriff in Prattsville let him go only to rearrest him later when Ulster County lawmen wanted to question him. His account was published in the newspaper as follows:

> *I went to find a place to sleep...I was just enjoying a beautiful nap when I heard someone come into the barn and the next thing I knew a couple of fellows with a big gun that looked like a cannon were telling me to hold up my hands. Did I hold them up? You bet I did. You would too if you saw that gun.*

O'Brien was brought to Kingston but was eventually let go when it became obvious, once again, that he was not Cooley. At this point, the case went cold.

Portsmouth is a town in New Hampshire along the Atlantic Coast. It is where a man who referred to himself as John Babbitt discovered that he had tuberculosis and was told that he did not have long to live. Babbitt was a resident of the New Hampshire State Hospital for the Insane. He was sent there for slashing his cellmate in jail and trying to take his own life afterward.

After being committed, Babbitt decided to attend a religious service at the asylum. His past had been bothering him as of late, and perhaps it was time to make peace with his maker for the horrible life he had led. When he returned to his quarters, Babbitt asked workers at the hospital to contact the local sheriff's department because he had something he needed to confess before he passed away. When Deputy Sheriff E.B. Shaw came to see the dying man, Babbitt told him that he had committed a murder about four years earlier in Highland, New York, in Ulster County. He had robbed eighteen dollars from a woman named Emma Brooks and then killed her by slashing her throat. Babbitt continued telling the deputy that he not only intended to murder Brooks but also wanted to obliterate Bragg, though he never had the chance. Babbitt was the Cooley authorities were looking for, though he claimed he never went by that name.

After taking down Babbitt's admission, Shaw contacted Ulster County authorities and explained whom they had in custody. The Monday following his statement, Babbitt escaped from the hospital with another man by cutting out the screen from the window in their room. They made it only a few miles from the asylum, to Concord, New Hampshire, where they were apprehended by police.

Undersheriff Dummond arrived in Concord on March 16, 1913. After interviewing Babbitt, he was convinced that this was Brooks's murderer. Babbitt knew too many of the intricate details of how the crime took place, including that it had initially been a robbery. When Brooks refused to hand over her money, there was a struggle, and Babbitt grabbed a knife and killed her. He claimed that he expected Brooks to have more than eighteen dollars, but that was all he was able to find. As far as the knife, he admitted to taking it off the kitchen table and tossing it under Brooks's stoop when the deed was done.

Shortly after taking Brooks's life, Babbitt met a man on a train, also a tramp, with whom he had been seen previously. Babbitt stated the man's name was Jack. He offered a description of the individual, which Dummond believed to be that of Cooley. The authorities had been looking for the wrong man. Babbitt inquired about "Jack" (Cooley) and hoped he was not arrested for the crime; he was assured that he wasn't.

After meeting with authorities in New Hampshire, Dummond requested that Babbitt be extradited back to Ulster County to stand trial for the murder of Brooks. He did not know if his request for extradition would be honored, as Dummond was told that Babbitt would first have to go to trial for his crimes of slashing his jail cellmate's throat and then cutting his own throat in a suicide attempt. In the end, Babbitt was never brought back to Ulster County for trial; in July 1913, he died from tuberculosis.

6

BAD, BAD WILLIE BROWN AND THE MONK EASTMAN GANG

Willie Brown hailed from New York City, where he boasted, to anyone who would listen, that he once was a member of the Monk Eastman Gang. No one could confirm this, but one thing was for sure—he made a life out of hustling and thievery. In the winter of 1908, "Brownie," as his friends called him, had come to Brown's Station, Camp 83, to kill a man, maybe two if the opportunity presented itself. However, in the end he would kill the wrong man.

As New York City continued to grow in the late nineteenth century and into the early twentieth century, so did the demand for water for its citizens. They needed not only water but also a clean source of it. Fostering this growth was wave after wave of immigrants. Officials in New York City decided that the cheapest and most logical place to obtain pure water was from the Catskill Mountains in upstate New York. The resulting Ashokan Reservoir quickly became the largest man-made lake in Ulster County.

A *Hudson Valley Magazine* article by A.J. Loftin placed the whole endeavor into perspective: "1,000 acres of farm land vanished…Eleven villages were forcibly evacuated and burned to the ground to make room for the 83,000-acre body of water—at the time, the world's largest reservoir." In short, all vestiges of these villages had to be eradicated, which demanded a massive amount of labor.

Loftin wrote, "A workers' camp rapidly arose on the southern slope of Winchell Hill near the town of Brown's Station. The camp had running water, electricity, paved streets, a sewage disposal plant, a hospital, and

Building the Ashokan Reservoir for a thirsty New York City attracted many "undesirables" to Ulster County. Most were there to work, but some were there to take advantage of the workers. *A.J. Schenkman's collection.*

garbage collection. It became customary for locals to drive to the camp on Sundays to inspect their odd new neighbors."

Camp 83 was one of the many "cabins" that dotted the landscape. They were built on the Ashokan for men working to supply water to a thirsty New York City. Specifically, Camp 83 was erected for employees of McArthur Brother and Winston, contractors hired by New York City for the construction of this mammoth project. The camp housed several men in three rooms.

In theory, the behavior of the workers was controlled not only by the management of the contractors but also by the Aqueduct Police. Alcohol, as well as any form of gambling, was strictly forbidden in Camp 83. Still, many men broke these laws, even under the penalty of a fine that could be as steep as "$3.30." This would cut deeply into workers' already meager wages. However, if they could keep their games under wraps and not attract too much attention, they usually would not get pinched by the Aqueduct Police. In December 1908, that was exactly what some men had hoped to accomplish in order to pass a cold night.

Enter Willie Brown. By all accounts, he did not work for McArthur Brother and Winston, but he claimed to be best friends with one of their workers, who went by the name of Joseph Lawson. Lawson was running a craps game

The Aqueduct Police tried their best to keep alcohol and gambling out of the camps around the Ashokan. They dealt with murders, assaults and gun possessions on a daily basis. *Courtesy of the Library of Congress.*

"Old Sparky"—the electric chair in Sing Sing Correctional Facility in Ossining, New York. *Courtesy of the Library of Congress.*

Sing Sing Correctional Facility in Ossining, New York, where Willie Brown and Monk Eastman were incarcerated. *Courtesy of the Library of Congress.*

that night. Later, in testimony, Brown declared that he had served time in Sing Sing prison in Ossining, New York, as he took the blame for a crime that Lawson had committed. Never one to rat on a friend, Brown served time for Lawson's infraction. In addition to doing time in Sing Sing, Brown bragged that he was also a member of the feared Monk Eastman Gang.

"Monk" Eastman was born on the Lower East Side of New York City. Some believe that the name "Monk" was short for "Monkey," as this is how many people described him due to the way his face looked after years of beatings and street fights. It is possible that Eastman recruited Brown for the gang, but in the winter of 1908, Eastman was in jail and would not reemerge permanently until 1917. His power by this time was no longer a factor.

It should be noted that some gangs employed other individuals to conduct their dirty work rather than their own members. Sometimes thugs like Brown claimed membership to strike fear and respect in others. Brown maintained that while he was in the gang, he was known as the "Yellow Kid"; this was a reference to his light skin color.

When Brown entered Camp 83 during the night of the game, it was late. The other men in the cabin had already started competing in craps.

Craps was a popular game that children and adults played. It was illegal in the camps where individuals labored while building the Ashokan. *Courtesy of the Library of Congress.*

Specifically, they were spread about the floor playing "show-down." When "the flashy dressed" Brown entered the cabin, the workers acknowledged him and continued on with their game.

Brown observed them for a period of time before deciding to place a five-cent bet, which he promptly lost. Brown was undeterred and followed up his initial bet with a fifty-cent bet, and he lost yet again. This signaled the start of trouble, as Brown began arguing with a man by the name of Eugene Herndon over his losses. The men were able to quiet the dispute.

Brown's buddy Lawson casually asked what led him to visit "the middle of nowhere" from New York City. Brown's answer—to kill a man—was simple, and that man was present at the craps game. His name was Quire Mitchell. Brown was offended by Mitchell telling him that if he hurt Herndon, Brown would have him to contend with. Brown did not take Mitchell's threat lightly and exclaimed that he could beat them both up, at the same time, without a problem. Lawson ushered Brown out of the game in an attempt to calm his friend and prevent violence from erupting.

When the two men returned to the camp, they went into a back room to talk. Lawson fixed his friend a plate of "sausage and rice." The craps game continued on, and Brown once again placed a bet. This time, he wagered twenty-five cents, which he also lost. Brown exploded and yelled at Mitchell that he was "going to kill him before morning."

Lawson asked to speak with Brown in a side room where there was, unbeknownst to them, a man sleeping. According to later testimony, the man overheard Lawson tell his friend to "knock it off." He was trying to discourage Brown from yapping about killing and asserted that no slaughters would occur that night. After assuring Lawson that he would settle down and cease the murder chatter, the pair reentered the gambling room.

In open defiance of Lawson, Brown promptly commenced voicing his murderous intentions and caused quite a scene. Finally, Lawson, who was larger than Brown, lost his cool and confronted him in front of everyone at the game. He stated:

> *See here, now, you've been making a disturbance all evening. I've tried to keep you quiet and you won't keep still. Now, you little ———, I can lick you up from the nub.*

He was answered by Brown, who called him "a liar."

Lawson then advanced on Brown with intentions of punching him, but before he was able to connect, Brown took out a revolver that he had borrowed earlier and fired at Lawson. The first bullet missed its target; however, the second bullet hit Lawson in his leg. It was such a close shot that the powder ignited Lawson's pants. The other men scattered after the first shot and ran to the door and windows. Lawson retreated to one of the rooms where he had spoken to Brown earlier and bellowed, "Brownie, you've shot me!" Brown responded, "Joe, are you shot? Joe, I wouldn't shoot you; I'm the best friend you have on this earth." Lawson replied, "Yes, Brownie, you've shot me, see?" Lawson would later die from the wound.

Hearing the commotion, Officers Edward Smith and John P. Dorsey of the Aqueduct Police arrived at the cabin. They arrested Brown and some of

Chain gangs sometimes awaited those who were sent to prison to do hard labor. *Courtesy of the Library of Congress.*

the other men as witnesses. A trial ensued, presided over by Judge Cantine. It took a short a period of time for the jury to supply a guilty verdict for murder in the second degree.

After a trial that lasted for about a week, Brown was convicted on March 22, 1909. He was sentenced to twenty years to life in Dannemora Prison. During the fall of 1909, Brown asked to be pardoned for the killing of Lawson; he even promised that he would never kill again. It made for interesting reading in the papers, but the pardon was denied.

7
I THINK I MAY HAVE HIT HIM

Louis Victor Seydel (also referred to as "Seydell"), a stockbroker in New York City, was also a Spanish-American War veteran. The successful Seydel lived with his family in a "top floor apartment in Crescent Court at 195 Claremont Ave." A thriving business allowed him to purchase some two acres of land on the Esopus Mountain in West Park, which was situated along the western shore of the Hudson River. It was on this land that Seydel contracted, in 1908, to have a two-story home built to serve as a summer residence from May to the end of August. One of his closest neighbors was John Burroughs, who also had a rustic retreat he called Slabsides.

In May 1910, just as in previous years, Seydel; his wife, Cornelia; and their two children, Frances and Louis Victor Jr., made their way up to their secluded mountain retreat. This summer would be much different than the previous ones.

Clements Demaron, at five feet, nine inches and 210 pounds, was an imposing figure. An Italian immigrant who originally settled New York City, he lived and thrived in West Park for almost twenty years. He was a well-respected businessman who, along with his wife Bridget, owned a hotel called the Demaron Hotel. When not running his hospitality business, Demaron sometimes furnished laborers for various projects that were emerging on the old Sherwood property on Esopus Mountain. Wealthy individuals, such as Seydel, had started building summer homes on these mountains. Many times, Demaron hauled supplies up the side of the mountain with his wagon and horse team.

Demaron, forty-five, and Seydel, thirty-eight, had never met each other before their paths crossed as each went about his life on the mountain on the morning of July 23, 1910. Fate is a funny thing, as their paths crossed as each went about their lives on the mountain on the morning of July 23, 1910. They met again on July 24, 1910, also in the morning. However, after the latter chance encounter, only one man walked off the mountain.

Seydel's bungalow was situated on two acres filled with a combination of primary and secondary trees with thick brush. Seydel made it a point to clear his property by removing trees that prohibited light from shining on the front lawn he had planted near a private road that ran up the mountain. During his two years in the area, he created a flower bed with the most sunlight; newspaper accounts relayed that the flowers were mostly asters. In addition to flowers, he also planted a vegetable garden, which he used to feed his family all summer long.

According to court records, an altercation surfaced when Demaron, constructing a house near Seydel's, noticed something disturbing while he was hauling "plaster boards" for wall construction. He observed that the horses that were hauling loads up the steep mountain road were exhausted. Demaron wanted to give the animals a rest. He instructed the driver, Louis Tironi, along with some others, to unload some of the boards from their wagon.

Seydel claimed that the men proceeded to place the boards in his flower garden. Seydel flew out of his home and told the driver not to place them on his flowers but to put them somewhere else on the property. Some reports state that the contractors ignored Seydel and continued up the mountain with a lighter load. When they returned to get the rest of the boards, Demaron and Seydel exchanged words; Seydel later alleged that Demaron threatened to "fix him." The two men and the driver parted ways. They met again the following day on the same stretch of road.

On Sunday morning, July 24, Demaron and several other men appeared with their team of horses to continue transporting boards to their work site. They made frequent stops, according to a newspaper reporter, with Demaron walking behind the wagon "carrying a stone"—he used this to chuck the wheels when the horses had to stop, which also prevented the wagon from rolling backward. When they passed Seydel's home, Seydel was outside and told them that the road was private and that they could not use it. Other roads could have been utilized, but this road was the easiest for the horses. Demaron also believed that this road was public.

During a later trial, Seydel's legal team asserted that it was within their client's purview to deny a right of way to Demaron. Property, they maintained, was a sacred right in the United States. Therefore, if Demaron and his crew continued their path, they would be trespassing on private property. According to witnesses, Demaron was not about to listen to Seydel and was determined to resume going up the mountain. A confrontation ensued with Seydel claiming that he feared for his life as the men got closer to him. His wife and children were in the house, and he felt obliged to protect them.

Men working for Demaron remembered that Seydel disappeared into his home and then emerged with a large revolver in his hand. When he approached Demaron, he was still loading the gun. Seydel's wife claimed that she had secured a big knife to be used to help her husband when she heard a commotion from her second-floor bedroom. Though early testimony disclosed that she yelled, "Don't shoot!" to her husband, Seydel's wife later contrarily stated that she in fact said, "Oh, Victor! Shoot! Shoot!" During her deposition, she could not remember if she was thinking this or if she actually said the words aloud.

Seydel was impelled to shoot because he believed that Demaron had a large rock in his hand, though some remember that Demaron had reached to the ground for a rock and was shot dead before he was able to do anything with it. The first shot pierced Demaron in his heart, causing him to drop in his tracks; a second shot became lodged in his leg. Demaron's workers scattered as they observed their boss falling into a crumpled heap in the road.

When one worker was approached by Seydel, he asked him for a glass of water. Seydel responded by telling him to go up to his house. Perhaps using this as a ruse to get away from the "killer," the man fled instead. Demaron's other workers ran down the road and did not stop until they reached West Park. Meanwhile, Seydel walked over to Demaron's lifeless body, and realizing that he was not going anywhere anytime soon, he stuck the .44 weapon "in his pocket, and started walking to West Park while his wife went off to church." During her deposition, Seydel's wife recalled that it was 10:00 a.m. at this time.

Newspapers reported that for some reason, Seydel thought he had to go to Poughkeepsie to give himself up to the sheriff there. However, in later articles, it was believed that he was going to Poughkeepsie because he had friends there whom he believed could assist him and put him in touch with proper representation. Law enforcement affirmed that they checked all records of individuals crossing the Hudson River at Highland. Seydel confirmed that he made no attempt to conceal himself during travel and used his own name in every direction. He added that the only stop he made was to the home of a neighbor, Mr. Seeley. After confessing to Seeley what

Cars made police officers' lives much easier. They allowed them to set up patrols and arrive at incidents faster. *Courtesy of the Library of Congress.*

he had done, he asked the man to drive him to Highland. From there, Seydel continued on to Poughkeepsie.

Seydel never turned himself in but instead visited an old friend named Mr. Booth, who took him to his lawyer. After listening to Seydel's story, the lawyer insisted that he give himself up in Ulster County instead of Dutchess County, as that is where the crime had been committed. The lawyer also offered to introduce Seydel to an excellent Kingston lawyer named Judge Clearwater. He felt that the judge would offer sound representation and would help him arrange for bail. By the time that Seydel arrived in Kingston and met with Clearwater, however, the judge informed him that Demaron had died from his wounds. This now meant that Seydel was a murderer; his head began to spin at the prospect.

While Seydel was meeting with Clearwater early Sunday afternoon, Undersheriff McLaughlin had been notified about the shooting. He assembled a few men, including Jailer Jocelyn, and they drove out to West Park to apprehend Seydel. When they arrived, he was nowhere to be found. Hours later, they found out that Seydel had surrendered to Clearwater and was then taken to Police Justice McKenzie a short distance away in Port Ewen.

Clearwater had also called Ulster County district attorney Cunningham to inform him of Seydel's crime and to assure him that he was in "custody." He asked Cunningham if he wished to examine Seydel; Cunningham responded

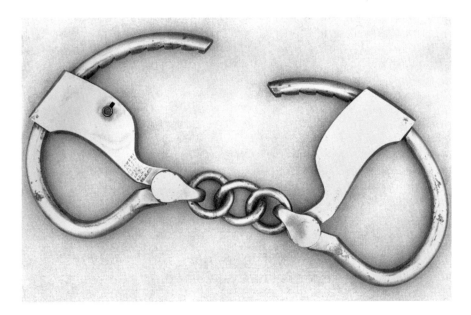

An earlier example of handcuffs carried by police officers when they apprehended criminals—even handcuffs did not slow them down for long. *Courtesy of the Library of Congress.*

that his assistant district attorney, who was in charge of such matters, was out of town. Cunningham would waive this right if the prisoner also agreed. By this time, a Sheriff Hoffman wanted to take Seydel into custody at once, but he was told that this was unnecessary.

After police court, the judge, along with several other individuals, went to West Park where the crime had been committed. Seydel, McKenzie and Clearwater then met with Constable Baker. Baker swore out a complaint against Seydel, which led to a warrant for his arrest for murdering Demaron. Baker then promptly detained Seydel. The party, with Seydel in irons, returned to Port Ewen, where he was arraigned before McKenzie. Seydel was committed to jail at seven o'clock in the evening with one request: he did not wish to make bail but would rather remain in jail.

By July 26, Seydel was still incarcerated. As stated in one paper, he did not wish to make bail because he feared for his life. He worried that Demaron's friends would exact vengeance on him. He was visited frequently by newspaper reporters, though, and when he wasn't talking to visitors, he wrote letters to his family.

A *Kingston Daily Freeman* reporter wrote about being frustrated over Seydel's refusal to talk about his pending case. One thing was for sure—his anti-Italian comments did not endear him to the slain man's friends or family. He

Police station where many criminal investigations started. *Courtesy of the Library of Congress.*

spoke in the papers about the excitability of Italians and that he feared them in a group but not as individuals. He also referred to Demaron, and the men who accompanied him, as "hot blooded Southern Italians…and as bad a class of people as you want to meet."

Alternately, he repeatedly stated that he regretted the death of the man, but he maintained that his life had been truly in danger, as well as those of his family. Although originally he had claimed in the newspapers that his wife and children were on an excursion in the mountains, he later contradicted himself by stating that they were in fact at home. Seydel related that he spoke to them before he left for Poughkeepsie to supposedly turn himself in, after meeting with friends who could help him.

A coroner's inquest was held on July 27 by Ulster County coroner Alexander Hasbrouck, at Demaron's Hotel (which was also known as the West Park Hotel). Once the examination had been completed, a funeral commenced in the front room of the hotel where Demaron's body was located. After services concluded, Demaron's family hoped to take possession of his body and accompany it by train to New York City, where he could be buried with family.

On August 6, Seydel's wife was examined by the District Attorney's Office. She was described by the papers as having "rebellious brown hair" with large brown eyes and a slight build and as being "prepossessing," or attractive. During the questioning, she told those assembled, including the Ulster County district attorney, that she did not know Demaron.

During the time of the murder, Seydel's wife claimed to have returned to her home in West Park from an outing to Poughkeepsie. She had her husband bring packages that she bought up to her house by way of a pony-drawn cart; she then had them placed under a tree. She left them there until she had time to get them because she needed to feed the couple's baby. She believed this to be at about 5:20 p.m. on a Saturday. When she came out to retrieve her packages, she remembered seeing a team of horses in the roadway that ran near their home. She noticed that her husband was talking to some men, including Demaron, in the street. The men who were in charge of the horse team and wagon were walking in her husband's flower beds.

On Sunday, the day of the shooting, she stated that she was preparing for church when she heard shouting coming from outside. When she looked out of a window, she claimed that her husband was engaged in a dispute with some of the men from the previous day. It was her opinion that his life was in danger, judging by all the swearing, as well as her husband's voice, which was angry. She stated that in case she needed to help her husband, she went to the kitchen to procure a carving knife. At that point, she remembered that Seydel entered the house and exclaimed that Demaron was outside; he then removed a revolver from his suitcase.

Seydel's wife recalls pleading with her husband to do "something" as he exited the house. By then, the men with Demaron dotted their front lawn, and Demaron held a large rock in his hand. Shortly after this scene, her husband shot the man.

A trial opened up on December 12, 1910, with Clearwater and Senator Linson mounting a vigorous defense of Seydel. They claimed that their client had defended his home against invasion and was not only protecting himself but also defending his family from the trespassing Demaron. They added that Demaron had been shot once before and had also been in trouble for bootlegging when Port Ewen was a dry town. However, he was never convicted.

After the trial, Clearwater would refer to his defense as "a man's home is his castle, and he has every right to defend it." This was an ancient law of every civilization. Cunningham, representing the deceased, wondered whether a Spanish-American War veteran like Seydel could have been that threatened. He also refuted that the shot that killed his late client was merely a lucky shot.

He countered Seydel's claims that he did not receive any training in the use of revolvers and felt that Seydel was well aware of how to use a gun, as he had been taught how to do so. He went as far as to say that Seydel had ample time to calculate what he was doing and realize the consequences of his actions.

Some witnesses suggested that Demaron only reached for a stone when he saw Seydel loading his .44. However, no one was sure if he actually picked up the stone before the gun was fired. Little Joe Marchesi, a young child who had witnessed the incident, gave a testimony about the rock, which was not admitted as evidence. According to the newspaper, the only evidence accepted was that offered by Seydel and his wife, who were referred to as "intensely interested parties."

In late December 1910, a jury delivered a verdict of not guilty of manslaughter "on the second ballot" to Judge LeBeouf. It took under two minutes for the jury to reach their decision. Reporters wrote that spectators in the court rose to their feet and applauded. The clapping was "led by ex-sheriff Zadoc P. Boice." On December 19, 1910, Seydel left the courthouse as a free man for the first time since July.

Shortly after the trial, on December 22, 1910, Seydel and his wife left where she had been staying on Green Street in Kingston and returned to New York City. Their plan, as reported in the paper, was to set sail for Bermuda. Once in Bermuda, they would spend some time recuperating from the long ordeal of the trial. However, Seydel was first served papers in a civil suit by Demaron's wife to recover damages resulting from the death of her husband.

The following summer, in 1911, the Seydel family was back in the Hudson Valley. They had sold their summer home and were visiting some of their friends in Poughkeepsie and around the area. In addition, Seydel decided to close down his stock-trading business in New York City. He did not speak about what he planned to do in the future or if he was even intending on remaining in New York City. Perhaps he might return to Indiana, where he was born. With the trial now behind the family, it would be a place to start anew. This apparently became the plan.

About seven years later, the *Kingston Daily Freeman* published a story that in July 1918, Seydel and his family were visiting in Kingston on their way to drop off their daughter at Wellesley College. It turns out that he did not return to his state of birth, but rather he settled in Grand Rapids, Michigan, where he was a businessman. According to the 1920 federal census, he lived in that city's second ward. Curiously, his occupation is listed as "none" in the same census. Demaron's wife, it seems, did not remain in West Park. She died three years later, in 1921, while in New York City.

8
BOYS WILL BE GIRLS AND GIRLS WILL BE BOYS

High Falls had its gamblers, pickpockets and gin joints, and they seemed to be concentrated on Pistol Row. It is here where Sarah Long made her presence known. When she walked down the street, there was no mistaking her 250-pound frame. Those unlucky enough to catch her gaze were quickly given the choice of giving up their money or receiving a quick beating. Men joked that with one punch, she could knock a man ten feet through the air. They refused to reciprocate because they felt that she was, after all, a woman. Most times, she sought out men who owed money to her or her husband, Neal Deace. However, George Thomas, a resident of Pistol Row, brought Long's reign to an end.

Long hailed from North Carolina. When exactly she met her husband is lost to time, but we know that the couple originally lived in Westchester and then later resided in Putnam County. When work became available on the New York Aqueduct from the accompanying project of building the Ashokan Reservoir, the two opened up a boardinghouse sometime around 1909. While Long maintained the day-to-day operations of the boardinghouse and its occupants, her husband was a day laborer.

Around that time, Long became known to the Aqueduct Police for running a disorderly house. She was sentenced, in March 1909, to three months in the Ulster County Jail; however, due to a mixup with the paperwork that was discovered by her counsel, she served only four weeks. Once free, Long returned to High Falls, where her husband still found employment digging the aqueduct until he fell ill.

Aqueduct Police Headquarters. Many of the officers in High Falls were battle-hardened army veterans who had seen fighting during the Spanish-American War. *Courtesy of the Library of Congress.*

When Long arrived to work in place of her husband, in order to keep his job, no one took much notice that she was dressed like, and kind of resembled, a man. The other laborers worked alongside her and thought nothing of it when she refused a medical exam and abruptly quit. The men she toiled with felt that it was her prerogative to do so, as a woman.

Long returned to her boardinghouse, where she looked after residents and walloped those who missed payments with her "fists as large as a lard pail and her muscles like iron." Once someone missed a rent payment to Long, the tenant never made the same mistake again after being on the receiving end of her temper. Male boarders mumbled under their breath that she was lucky she was a woman.

Long's issue with Thomas, whom she called Blue, is not known. One day, the two stood in the middle of Pistol Row at 4:15 p.m. yelling at each other. Having tired of Thomas, Long picked up an ax and took a swing at him. Before Long could reach her target, Thomas pulled out a .32-caliber revolver and pointed it directly at her; she was undeterred. In a flash, the revolver exploded and sent a bullet smashing through Long's skull,

One of the many homes in Brown's Station near the Ashokan, which was one of the more notorious areas surrounding the worksite. *A.J. Schenkman's collection.*

entering above her left eye and coming to rest in her brain. The shooting aroused the police, who came running in force to the notorious Pistol Row. They found Long lying facedown with blood pouring out of her wound; Thomas had fled.

Police brought Long to the T.A. Gillespie Company Hospital, where she was attended to by the local doctor, Frank Johnson. It was believed that she would be dead before the morning. Long was unconscious, but she awoke briefly and witnessed the doctor and his associates standing beside her bed. Their eyes were wide open, and their mouths agape. She gazed at them and then down at her own body: she was naked. Long tried to cover herself up but then lost consciousness again. As she was fading, she heard someone exclaim: "She is a man!"

As Johnson regained his composure after this latest turn of events, Aqueduct police officer Joseph Michels had caught up with Thomas. He arrested him on the towpath near Rosendale. Thomas was told that the woman he shot was in fact John Flemming; he then became quiet and refused to discuss why he shot the woman he knew as Long.

While Thomas was brought to jail for questioning, Long battled for her life. She once again regained consciousness, and a few days later, she was talking and eating as if she had no trauma unleashed on her brain. The bullet, however, was still lodged in her head. Thus, the doctors, including one from Stone Ridge, decided to drill into her head in an effort to remove the bullet.

Everyone marveled at Long's recovery; other than some paralysis on the left side of her face, she seemed unaffected by her wound. She was willing to talk about any topic that the doctors or visitors asked her about, with the exception of why she dressed as woman. Some of the few facts they managed to cull from her were that she was from North Carolina and had

Superintendent of the Aqueduct Police on horseback; horses were still the most efficient way to patrol. *Courtesy of the Library of Congress.*

been wearing women's clothing for some eighteen years. As for Thomas, he once again refused to reveal anything about the altercation with Long.

Through mid-August 1909, doctors continued to attend to Long; they even had to remove a blood clot from her brain. Johnson, who originally treated Long, along with Dr. Edward Peck and Dr. Sherman of Stone Ridge, assisted in the operation. They remarked that after this latest procedure, Long's paralysis was much improved, as was her speech. However, Long refused to implicate Thomas or discuss a possible motive behind the shooting. Doctors were hoping to discharge her when she suddenly took a turn for the worse. On August 20, 1909, she died from a cerebral hemorrhage…or did she?

The *Kingston Daily Freeman* reported that Ulster County was under the impression that the woman Long, otherwise known as the man Flemming, had perished. Shockingly, it then discovered that she was not deceased but

Police barracks at Brown Station near the Ashokan Reservoir construction site. *A.J. Schenkman's collection.*

was serving time in prison in November 1909—three months after her death was reported in the newspapers. Some believed that a Mr. Bensel, who was running as the Democratic nominee for state engineer, "resurrected" her. Many felt that Bensel wanted to show potential voters that as president of the water board, he was tough on the rampant crime occurring around the reservoir project, especially in High Falls and Brown's Station. It is more than likely that Bensel never realized that Long had been pronounced dead. As for Thomas, he never spoke a word about the murder, and the newspapers soon lost interest in him and Long.

Part II
MAYHEM

9

A PEACEFUL MASTICATION

From the late 1800s right on up to the early 1900s, newspapers started to generate interest in what they called "the curiosity from the south." They were talking about alligators, which many people enjoyed keeping as pets. A problem occurred, however, when they became too big to possess; they were then either butchered for meat, shot or let go into the nearest waterways. There is no record of what law enforcement tried to do to prevent people from bringing these reptiles to their homes and then letting them go.

Imagine the surprise of William Smith, of Sleightsburgh in Kingston, when he went out for a day of trapping muskrats along the Hudson River and came across an alligator while checking his traps. He believed the creature, which was sunning itself on a riverbank, to be three feet long. Smith, stunned and probably fearing for his safety, leveled his gun and promptly killed it.

In another instance, Company M, an infantry regiment stationed in Kingston, decided that an alligator from Florida would make a great mascot. When housing an alligator, even in an armory, the keepers have to ensure that its holding pen is secured. However, when someone arrived to feed the reptile, it was discovered that it had in fact escaped. Men from the company searched everywhere for it, as they worried that someone would be eaten or killed by their new mascot. It was eventually located in a pile of coal in the basement of the armory. This was not the only instance of these creatures finding their way into the most inopportune of places. Mr. Plepp, of the Morgan Turner Brickyard, located a three-foot alligator nestled in some bricks.

The most popular 'gators were those of A.H. Bruyn; he kept two of them behind a high board fence at the corner of Fair and Pearl Streets. Bruyn attempted to re-create an authentic environment for his pets with tropical plants and shrubs. There is no mention of what became of the reptiles during the harsh northern winters. This did not appear to be of interest to the Bruyns, though. Instead, they were concerned with the fuss their neighbors made over their creatures possibly escaping. Bruyn assured those around him that his reptiles didn't have the ability to climb and that they were quite secure in their bearings. His most pressing issue was that he could not keep up with the fresh supply of meat that the alligators demanded. Bruyn came up with a solution.

From reading old newspaper accounts, Kingston appeared to periodically have a problem with cats and dogs running rampant around the city. Many of these animals were sadly unwanted and were thus abandoned by their owners. Bruyn proposed what he thought was a novel approach to this issue: he requested that individuals cast the animals they no longer wanted over his fence for a "gentle and easy mastication." It turns out that the creatures were quite fond of dog, as well as cat, meat. Some people were afraid to feed the alligators their animals for fear of becoming meals themselves. Once again, Bruyn concocted a solution. The former pets or strays could be lowered into his alligators' pen by way of a leash or rope. He added that the 'gators would do the rest of the work.

Keeping 'gators as pets was not limited to Kingston. One woman in Pittsfield, Massachusetts, named Kathryn Wheeler sued her husband for divorce because he terrorized her with his pet alligator. At one point, the creature even bit her in the arm. Despite this uncomfortable fact, some women did keep 'gators as pets. This was the case with Miss Hotaling of Port Ewan.

A church function boasted that Hotaling was returning from a vacation in the "southern resorts" with a pet alligator in tow. What she did with the alligator after it became too difficult to handle is not known. It can be assumed, as with cases in Ellenville, that it was released and left to fend for itself.

It also appears that some individuals developed a taste for alligator meat. Some local butchers advertised carrying this delicacy especially for these people. Alligators also became used as fashion accessories for women. Susan B. Anthony, the famous suffragette, carried an alligator handbag and clutches. All of these unchecked factors, such as taking alligators as pets, hunting them for meat and fashion and the loss of their habitats, contributed to a marked decline of the alligator population, especially in Florida.

The days of finding alligators in the waterways of Ulster County are long gone. One of the reasons is that there are now strict laws prohibiting anybody from housing exotic animals or reptiles, such as 'gators, without a proper permit. Nowadays, these creatures, and in some cases the mayhem they created, are just a part of Ulster County's rich and colorful past.

10

BIG BAD BILL STRIKES AGAIN

Katie Davis-Monroe sat in her home and waited for the familiar car lights of lawmen to illuminate the road leading up to her house. Her new husband, Big Bad Bill Monroe, begged her to go on the run with him, but she refused. As expected, officers approached her place and demanded that Davis-Monroe reveal the whereabouts of her husband. She told them that he was around but had fled; she didn't know for sure where he was located. They searched in and around her house to no avail.

Monroe was a well-known individual when he made news in the summer of 1908; he was also a notorious figure to local law enforcement due to his violent temper. It was agreed by most that at some point, Monroe was going to kill someone—it was only a matter of time until he did. Suffice it so say, no one was really that surprised when he assaulted not just one member of the Deyo family but all six Deyos plus their farm workers. He then burned down their barn.

After the effects of the alcohol wore off, Monroe sat on the porch attached to his house and pondered his next move. He realized that the authorities would soon be coming for him. He decided that he would take off for the mountains to meet up with the rest of the Shawangunk Gang. Monroe eluded being caught, even after the town board of Gardiner posted a $100 reward for the capture of the twenty-five-year-old. Sheriff Boice of Ulster County also offered a reward of $300 for apprehending Monroe. A reward poster described him as five feet, six inches tall with light hair, a stout build, fair complexion, a tattoo of a star on his wrist and a mole on his left cheek. Twice

Sheriff Boice was feared and respected by the likes of Big Bad Bill and other notorious criminals. *Elizabeth Werlau's collection.*

wounded and pursued through two states by farmers and dogs, Monroe was seized as many times but escaped.

Although Davis-Monroe had not committed any crimes and had not been present at the Deyo home when Monroe attacked the family, the local constable, Charles Litts of New Paltz, decided to take her into custody. He housed her in the Ulster County Jail. Litts felt that the newlyweds would want to be together and that Monroe would most likely make his way back to his wife. In addition to serving as bait, having Monroe's wife in custody would also prevent her from joining her husband.

Ulster County undersheriff Dummond met Litts at the jail and told him that Davis-Monroe had done nothing wrong, so they could not forcibly keep her there, nor would he allow it. As a result, Monroe's wife was taken out of prison and placed instead in the jailer's apartment. Periodically, she was asked questions about Monroe. She assured authorities that she had no intention of meeting up with the "Gardiner Desperado," as he had come to be known. However, she was content to wait for him in the jailer's apartment. Eventually, though, Davis-Monroe decided to return to her home. As she departed, she requested that the authorities inform her when they caught her husband so that she could see him.

There is not really much known about Davis-Monroe. She was young when she met Monroe—the newspapers claimed that she was sixteen years old and was the daughter of "Little Dan" Davis. When she realized, after her husband had finally been captured, that he would not be home anytime soon, she relocated to her grandmother's home in Middletown, New York.

Violence plagued Davis-Monroe. When her husband drank, he became brutal toward her. In 1910, she found herself in a dangerous situation with another drunken man when she was at her grandmother's house.

Officer Louis Roth, out on morning patrol, found a young woman shivering and covered from head to toe with mud and slush. When he asked her name, she replied "Katie Davis-Monroe" and stated that she was staying with her grandmother, Mrs. George Smith. She explained that she had been looking for a police officer and quickly recounted the ordeal she had just endured. Davis-Monroe claimed to have walked three miles by the time Roth encountered her on the corner of North Street.

Her story unfolded: While at her grandmother's home, a knock came at the door. Smith opened it, and there stood Charles Osborne. Osborne was listed in the 1910 census as a farm laborer who was married with a stepdaughter. He was known to become aggressive when he drank, which was often. It is not clear if Smith made the mistake of letting Osborne into her home or if he forced his way in. Once inside, however, he tried to assault Davis-Monroe while her grandmother attempted to prevent this from occurring.

Unfazed, Osborne picked up an ax near the fireplace and swung it at Smith. He rapped her on the side of the head. Davis-Monroe fled the home while looking back to see blood streaming from the crumbled figure that was her grandmother.

Big Bad Bill must have known this room, the Dannemora Prison mess hall, well. *Courtesy of the Library of Congress.*

Roth took Davis-Monroe to the Hotel Waldo. He instructed her to remain there until the morning. After daybreak, they returned to her grandmother's house to swear out a warrant for the arrest of Osborne. When Monroe finally returned to his wife, the brutality in her life continued.

Monroe rejoined his wife after he was released from Dannemora. He served what was almost a four-and-a-half-year sentence there. Some say that he was even fiercer and meaner than when he went into prison. While in Dannemora, Monroe's problem was summed up in one word: "rowdyism." He worked in the knit factory and was constantly fomenting strikes and even riots. He was quickly identified as a ringleader.

The reason for these uprisings is unknown, but it could have been due to the bad conditions at the prison. A *New York Times* article from 1911 discussed that in the knitting room where Monroe worked, two foremen were dismissed for allowing prisoners access to everything, from revolvers to even dynamite. Both were used in unsuccessful escape attempts from the prison.

A riot in April 1911 resulted in the near death of a guard, Officer Barret, who was attacked by Monroe when his back was turned. Barret retaliated by giving Monroe two bullet holes in order to save his own life. He was also assisted by an inmate, Chas Chaffee, who was eventually pardoned by Governor Dix for his

Sing Sing Correctional Facility warden James M. McClancy. *Courtesy of the Library of Congress.*

heroic efforts. When it had become clear that Dannemora needed to be rid of the Gardiner Desperado so that order could be restored, he was shipped to Sing Sing. This was determined to be the most logical place to send him, as Sing Sing was known for reducing even the hardest men to rubble.

During the summer of 1912, Big Bad Bill Monroe was in Sing Sing, where he met an even more unscrupulous man than himself. This man was the noted Jewish gangster Nathan Kaplan, who was better known by his street name of Kid Dropper. Kaplan was a member of the Five Points Gang that ruled the streets of New York City. The group was infamous for being one of the most violent street gangs in the area.

The two men, along with a third troublemaker, created problems at Sing Sing that were similar to those that had plagued Dannemora. Another

A cartoon portraying the Sing Sing Correctional Facility Sanitarium in Ossining, New York. *Courtesy of the Library of Congress.*

guard, Officer Mullen, was stabbed and almost killed by Michael Barberis. Once again, Monroe was implicated. Thus, when Warden Kaiser was finally able to reestablish control over Dannemora, Monroe and seventy-five other prisoners from Sing Sing were shipped back to the upstate prison. This move was meant to help quell the problems now surfacing at Sing Sing. Though Monroe would be quiet for now, he'd also be plotting more mayhem and wickedness for his return to Ulster County a short time later.

When Monroe was released from prison in 1915, it did not take him long to find trouble again. This time, he joined his brother Albert in burglarizing the home of Maurice Minton of Dutchess County. They admitted to stealing "a stove, furniture, and food." Monroe's brother stashed the loot near the house where they were living "at the foot of Stormville Mountain." The Monroe brothers did not end up serving time for this crime but were instead granted probation as long as they agreed to stay out of Dutchess County. Though they both agreed to keep this promise, Bill did not heed it.

The brothers told their judge that they'd be leaving the state and heading to New Jersey. Monroe did not journey to Jersey, however, but landed in Highland Mills in Orange County, New York. It was here that he had a house and made headlines again. In order to cut down on pedestrian accidents in the area, workers were told to put in new sidewalks. One of these pavements was slated to be installed in front of Monroe's dwelling. He became incensed at this prospect and kept walking through the wet cement to prevent it from drying properly.

Monroe was eventually tackled by the foreman on the job. He, in turn, bit the man and drew blood. Monroe once again found himself being arrested and dragged before a judge. He was given a suspended sentence as long as he agreed to leave Highland Mills. This time, he kept his word and left.

The year 1916 would prove to be a busy one, legally speaking, for Monroe. He was arrested at least three times that year. During the third instance, he was apprehended by Sheriff Schultis, who was ordered to deal with Monroe once and for all. Monroe continued to wreak havoc, however, especially in the Ulster County town of Plattekill. Apparently, when Monroe returned from Dannemora, he reunited with his wife, and they settled down there.

One evening, Monroe and his wife had guests over at their Plattekill abode. Never one to forget his manners, when it became dark Monroe escorted one of his female guests back to her home. He instructed his wife to have dinner prepared upon his return. Instead, Davis-Monroe decided to visit a next-door neighbor. When her husband reappeared, he became enraged that she had disobeyed him. He proceeded directly to the house where his wife was socializing and kicked open the door. Before she had time to react, Monroe flew across the room and grabbed her around the throat. Witnesses recounted that his handprints could still be seen on her neck days later.

After almost killing his wife, or believing that he had in fact murdered her, Monroe broke everything in their home, including the cast-iron stove. After his orgy of violence, he calmly sat down on a broken piece of furniture to compose a note to his wife; he was leaving her forever. According to the papers of the day, he did indeed ditch his wife; he also continued to harass the residents of Plattekill, including employees at the White Cross Creamery—he walked into that establishment and started firing his gun in the air.

In order to apprehend Monroe for his latest escapades, the local sheriff, Undersheriff Hornbeck, and Night Jailer Jocelyn felt it would be safer to approach the outlaw at night. One newspaper printed that even though Monroe was quite the bandit, he respected local law enforcement and never put up a fight. It was also noted that he seemed to be on his worst behavior when in the vicinity of New Paltz and Plattekill.

The three lawmen and their deputies searched for Monroe "in his usual haunts, the trail led to Newburgh and then off to Rock Cut, to four miles west of Orange Lake where he was located." Expecting a fight, one of the sheriffs entered the tavern where Monroe was hanging out and ordered

The phone, like the car, made police work easier. Sheriff Boice telephoned Big Bad Bill at one point. *Courtesy of the Library of Congress.*

him to come along peacefully. Monroe acquiesced and even held out his hands so that the jailer could slap cuffs on him more easily. He was arraigned before Justice Ostrander and taken to the Ulster County Jail to await his court appearance.

Monroe's antics continued into 1917 and well into 1918. Every time he was arrested or convicted, he pleaded not guilty. Monroe claimed that he was driven to these delinquent behaviors, his victims deserved what they got or someone other than himself had committed the crime.

Monroe found himself in jail again for thirty days in Goshen, New York, for assault in the fall of 1917. This time, his crime was committed at the saloon of Henry J. Saunders on Fulton Street. While drinking at the pub, Monroe found himself in a "heated argument" with another patron. Perhaps knowing of Monroe's reputation and fearing that the situation could quickly escalate, Saunders intervened in order to separate the two men. Monroe, displeased at the interruption, picked up a chair and smashed it across Saunders's head. Even though Saunders was now lying unconscious on the floor, Monroe continued his argument. When he felt his speech was finally complete, he took off. He was released from jail in early December 1917.

After a short period of relative quiet, Monroe was again incarcerated in May 1918. Undersheriff Hallock of Orange County took Monroe into custody for allegedly robbing two farms in Cornwall. He was convicted on two counts of burglary. One of these crimes occurred in Mountainville, New York, where Monroe was keeping company with a person of interest who was wanted for questioning by the United States government. The person's name was Michael M. Meyers, a gentleman of German descent.

It was believed, for reasons not stated in the newspapers, that Meyers was a spy working for the Germans as World War I raged on in Europe. The two men ended up not being held on burglary charges but were charged with "handling explosives without a permit." Authorities tried to sort out all the stories surrounding Meyers and appeared to have less interest in Monroe, for once. They didn't even seem to care that he was now "shacked up" with his dead brother's widow. Patience was starting to wear thin with Monroe and his antics. He was finally sentenced to three years in Sing Sing Prison for numerous thefts in and around Cornwall. He was due to be discharged in the early years of the next decade; it appears that he was.

Monroe, now forty-four years of age, had only been out of jail for half a year when, along with his nephew Harold Barrett, he decided to pay a visit to the Fishkill Hermit. Monroe knew the hermit well, as he was his brother-in-law, Andrew Barrett. Monroe had been married to the hermit's late sister. It was rumored that Barrett kept many valuables, as well as cash, in his "shack" on the estate of the Countess d'Ivry.

Monroe almost beat the hermit to death just before going to prison. Prior to this incident, he had also mugged the man. A local newspaper reported that Monroe left a note for the hermit stating that he would return to take his money. When Monroe and his nephew arrived at the shack, he sprang into action and almost decapitated his former brother-in-law with one swing of an ax he had found. While the man lay dying, the duo tied him up with linens. They retrieved several thousands in cash and bolted. It was believed that they initially fled to Sullivan County in "a Ford" and proceeded to cross the state line into New Jersey, where they were caught. The two vagrants were brought to Poughkeepsie to stand trial. There had been a $500 reward for their capture.

The Gardiner Desperado was sentenced to twenty years to life for second-degree murder and was again carted off to Sing Sing. In November 1923, shortly after his sentence commenced, Monroe sent a letter to the District Attorney of Dutchess County proclaiming his innocence. He also offered to shed light on who had actually killed Barrett.

Monroe ended up pleading guilty, however, because he was terrified at the possibility of being sent to the electric chair. Monroe deemed that the prejudice against him was so immense that he was bound to be found guilty. However, Monroe was still able to convince a local lawyer of his possible innocence, as he claimed to have obtained a letter from the person who actually murdered the elder Barrett.

The solicitor who took up Monroe's cause was a former fellow convict named William H. Anderson. Anderson was a former Anti-Saloon League leader who truly felt that Monroe had been "railroaded." He continued to push for Monroe's release, even after repeated refusals by Governor Smith. Eventually, someone did grant Monroe freedom, as he was released from Sing Sing in the late 1920s.

Big Bad Bill Monroe, the Gardiner Desperado, appears to have learned his lesson after this latest conflict with the law. His name does not appear again in the local newspapers until the 1930s, when a body was located in a field in Plattekill that closely resembled that of Monroe. After the body was examined, it was declared by authorities that the individual resembled Monroe, but it was not him.

11

HANNAH MARKLE'S SALOON OF MURDER

The name Hannah Markle and her saloon, the Capital Café, at 70 North Front Street in the Old Stockade District in Kingston, New York, were on everybody's lips in the first decade of the twentieth century. If there was a murder, suicide, beating or a piano player mysteriously dropping dead after playing, chances are it originated at her establishment. For the Woman's Christian Temperance Union (WCTU), she was Public Enemy Number One; her pub was a subject of frequent meetings and police raids. The local newspapers of the day reported diligently on the sin that ran rampant through both day and night at her place.

Apparently, there was only one Hannah, and she was described as "short and fat." When newspaper headlines proclaimed an event "at Hannah's," there was no need to put in a last name. Even when she was arrested several times for keeping a "disorderly house," she seemed lucky enough to post bail. One particular incarceration seemed to be an attempt to keep her establishment closed during a planned celebration of the 250th anniversary of Kingston's founding. The judge set bail at "1,000," a phenomenal amount of money during that time period. Markle, of course, was able to post bail in time to celebrate with Kingston by having her "café" open.

One of the more tragic events at Hannah Markle's saloon involved a twenty-three-year-old woman named Lizzie Long. Although the papers did not explicitly state it, she was most likely a prostitute at the bar. In addition to other endeavors, Long was also involved in fencing stolen items from various houses that had been robbed by acquaintances. After receiving a tip, the

Early Kingston, New York—the scene of much murder and mayhem. One of the more notorious individuals of this time was Hannah Markle. *Courtesy of the Library of Congress.*

Kingston Police picked up one of Long's accomplices, who ratted her out. Police had reason to believe that she had sold stolen goods in a robbery that occurred on Lucas Turnpike. It was only a matter of time until the police appeared at her door to arrest her.

In the early morning hours of July 3, 1906, Long left with a Mr. Hornbeck to head back to her home in Rondout. Hornbeck remembered that he forgot something at the saloon and needed to go back to retrieve it. The two had gotten as far as Crown Street. The newspapers reported that Hornbeck then heard a shattering of glass, which turned out to be a vial of "carbonic acid"; he turned to see Long on the ground. When he arrived by her side, he could smell the acid fumes. A doctor was summoned, but it was too late. It was surmised that Long had committed suicide rather than face a certain fate of jail time for pushing stolen goods.

Markle's saloon was described as "not very wide but quite long." It was divided up into a "lower floor," which in turn was "divided into three rooms." The first room was utilized as a "bar room"; the others were referred to as "sitting rooms." In the corner of the main area of the bar sat Frank Sheldon, the piano player. He had been employed by Markle since March 1907. He

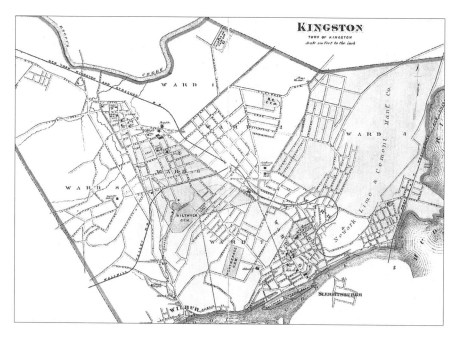

A map of Kingston from the 1875 county atlas of Ulster, New York. *Courtesy of the Ulster County Clerk, Archive Division.*

lasted only three months, dropping dead while playing the piano. A coroner believed that Sheldon had drunk himself to death.

In a packed saloon with alcohol flowing like water, there are bound to be problems. This held especially true in November 1907, as four men from the Rondout area of Kingston entered Markle's establishment. The men—Edward Leach, Henry Butler, "Bud" Dugan and John O'Brien—were no strangers to the pub. Some later agreed that the men were hoping for a fight that night, a wish that typically could easily be accommodated.

During this evening, Leach excused himself from the other three men to use the bathroom. Even though Leach had often been at the drinking establishment, he was unable to find the bathroom so he looked for someone to ask. Leach spotted a woman sitting on a whiskey barrel in a dark part of the saloon talking to a gentleman.

There were two "popular" women who frequented the saloon. They were known as Bertha "the Grand Old Rag" Acker and Emma Broadhead. Both women were rumored to be of ill repute. Leach made his way over to Acker and asked her where the restroom was located. She gladly gave Leach directions and pointed to the proper spot. Before heading to his destination, however, he threw Acker off the barrel for no reason. The man she was talking to, Harry Barnhart, unleashed a few insults at Leach, who then spun around and slapped Acker off the barrel she was perched on again. This was followed by more posturing by both men until patrons managed to diffuse the situation.

Leach finally made his way to the bathroom. While there, some witnesses to the previous altercations voiced their opinion that it just might be time to "clean house." This was a reference used by saloon regulars to clear out any troublemakers there. The front door was then locked so that no one could flee.

After the entrance was secured, almost on cue, bottles, chairs, spittoons, fists and whatever else that was not bolted down flew in all directions. A witness later reported that Markle and her bartender took refuge behind the bar with other patrons who did not want to partake in the mayhem. Unfortunately, there was no choice but to get involved.

While the hysteria ensued, Nicola Zolo and John Rosso sat at a table drinking beer behind a closed door. They became aware of the ruckus when someone shut off the lights and two fighting men crashed through the door behind which they were sitting. Zolo and Rosso looked at each other and drew their knives. They blindly slashed and stabbed in an attempt to make it through the crowd to the front door, which they found was locked. Finally, they saw a way to escape, as a front window had been shattered. Police later estimated that the brouhaha was over in less than ten minutes and involved over twenty people. The only person of the four men from Rondout who didn't end up being injured was Dugan. The other three men were bleeding heavily from their stomachs and sides from deep stab wounds. Markle suffered a cut to her face, and her bartender had several teeth knocked out in the fracas.

Police Officer William Ryan was the first official on the scene; he found the bar to be completely destroyed. He received a description from Leach of the man whom he believed had stabbed him. Ryan conferred with Detective Sergeant Cahill and Officers Shader and Murphy as Leach sought medical attention with his buddies. They went to Doctor Follette's, who, according to a local newspaper, had an office on Fair Street.

Once Leach et al arrived at the doctor's office, additional doctors were called in to assist Follette. The men's wounds bled so heavily that even with extra doctors, their injuries were difficult to treat in an office setting. An ambulance was summoned, and the three wounded men were transferred to Benedictine Hospital. They were operated on and remained in critical condition. Doctors expected Leach to die.

Using Leach's description of the attackers, the police located Zolo, believed to be an employee of the West Shore Railroad. They also found Rosso, employed by Campbell and Dempsey. The two were brought in for questioning at the police station. It was later ascertained that Rosso worked for the railroad, not Zolo. It was also discovered that a John Pallazzi was involved in the mêlée that night, not Rosso.

This latest pandemonium proved to be too much for Markle. She decided it would be best to surrender her license as a saloonkeeper. However, the pub remained open, as it was taken over by her bartender, James E. Herdsman Sr. The WCTU voiced disbelief that this house of debauchery was permitted to remain open when authorities finally had an opportunity to close it. It was more than likely that Herdsman was a front for Markle, who still ran the saloon and owned the building.

Some individuals never learn their lessons, and this became apparent with Leach. He was involved in another brutal fight a year and a half later, in May 1909, again at Markle's. This brawl involved well-known characters named "Toots" Delaney and James Stetson, who lived on Mill Street. Leach and Stetson, both drunk, got into an argument and decided to have a scrap away from any potential "witnesses." The best place they could think of was the "High Road." Stetson quickly got the best of Leach, until Delaney stepped in to help his friend. The skirmish continued as the men moved from the High Road to the Ulster and Delaware train yard where Delaney and Leach left Stetson unconscious. Stetson eventually recovered, and he promptly swore out a warrant for the arrest of his attackers.

One of the more interesting fights that occurred at Markle's involved Leo Moran. He was arrested for breaking the jaw of Arthur Ellsworth. When Ellsworth was questioned by the police, he stated that he was not really sure "who hit him, but he was sure where the fight took place." Despite this, Moran was arrested and charged with second-degree assault. His bail was set at "800 dollars, which Hannah Markle wanted to post but was denied."

Markle, who was not a young woman, became weary of the saloon and its violence. She also grew tired of being harassed for the notoriety her bar attracted. In September 1908, she decided to sell her place; it quickly was bought for "1400 dollars."

In June 1908, Markle decided to move from Kingston to Esopus. According to newspapers at the time, Esopus became a "wet" town, meaning that alcohol could be served there. Markle saw thirsty patrons as a potential business opportunity. There is no indication that she ever opened up a new saloon, especially since those in Esopus were probably not eager to have a woman with Markle's reputation open up an establishment.

Markle passed away in 1912. She left behind a last will and testament that granted all her personal belongings and real estate to her grandchildren: Irving, John and Catherine Egnor. Her grandsons were given cash and bedroom sets from the home she owned at 71 Crown Street. Her granddaughter was left the actual house and surrounding lot, along with the remainder of her personal effects. With her passing, the colorful story of Markle and her Capital Café came to an end.

12

JAILBREAKS

J ailbreaks capture the imagination of the public. There are numerous movies portraying the subject, such as *Escape from Alcatraz*. Early newspapers in Ulster County were no different, highlighting the problem in jails such as the one that sat on Wall Street in Kingston, New York. Hardly a Sing Sing, Dannemora or Alcatraz Island, the Ulster County Jail nonetheless had some interesting jailbreaks and at least one case of a person breaking into the jail.

Newspapers of the time were captivated by attempted escapes from prison, even when they were not in Ulster County. For example, "Cat Eye Annie," a notorious jewel thief who was described as the most dangerous woman in the country, made headlines for breaking out of the Auburn prison in central New York. It is important to point out that prisoners did not bust out often, but when they did, it was big news. More often than not, those who absconded were apprehended by the "sleuths" of the time. Ulster County sheriffs Zadoc P. Boice and "Fearless" Phil Schantz, along with Deputy Sheriff William Cohen, are just a few of the detectives who were infamous during the Ulster County Sheriff's Department's long history.

In 1903, a female inmate at the Ulster County Jail, Jennie Green, had the distinction of "being the first attempt at a break out since the new jail was erected and the old jail repaired." She did not quite break loose from the building but came close. Green was being housed in the women's part of the prison. How she was able to obtain a "clasp knife" is not known. She did realize at some point, while awaiting trial, that all of the walls that surrounded her were not reinforced with steel. With plenty of time to think

Wall Street in Kingston, New York. *Courtesy of the Library of Congress.*

The Ulster County Courthouse in Kingston, New York, where the murder and mayhem ended for many. *A.J. Schenkman's collection.*

and observe, Green discovered that one outside wall was made of plaster and lathe. A sharp blow from her tool confirmed this; she then went to work. Without being noticed initially, she was able to clear away the layers of plaster and lathe. She then faced a "seven to eight inch thick wall" made up of small stones. Once again with her tool in hand, Green hunkered down.

Jailer Carman, according to a local newspaper, became aware of an abundance of "falling mortar." He went to investigate the source. As he neared Green's cell, he heard a digging sound. When he peered inside, there was plaster and mortar all over the floor. He watched for a period of time, as the inmate was so consumed with excavating that she neglected to realize that she was being observed. Carman finally entered Green's cell—she was guiltily covered in plaster. He then moved her to a more secure unit until her arraignment the following day.

The week of August 22, 1897, was a warm one at the Ulster County Jail. When the jail heated up, it became very uncomfortable for the prisoners being housed. In order to show some compassion, jailers permitted inmates to sleep outside of their cells in the corridors. Once everything in the jail settled down for the night, and they were sure that the jailer was asleep, four prisoners implemented their escape plan.

Joseph Decker, William Lasher, John Boylan and Charles Sullivan had somehow secured a saw. As the jailer slept, they set to work on some inner iron bars. They then tackled a second set of bars on the outside wall at the rear of the jail. It is hard to believe that they didn't awaken anyone with all their noisy sawing. Jailer Smith was surprised when he was awakened and informed by a prisoner that the four men had escaped in the night. He went to investigate and found that four bars on each side of the wall had been cut, revealing a "fourteen inch square through which the prisoners escaped." All four inmates had lowered themselves from the second floor using a blanket.

There are other interesting jailbreaks in Ulster County, such as the one led by an individual named Thomas Cosgrove. He managed to pick the lock on his cell with a broken broom handle because the safety had not been set on the lock. Cosgrove, and two other escapees, was quickly apprehended. One of the three convicts was captured in Albany while doing his laundry on the banks of the Hudson River.

Escape efforts did not just occur in jails, however. For example, the Eastern New York Reformatory at Napanoch, which opened in 1900, encountered numerous flight attempts in its early history. One of the craftiest breakouts came from career criminal James "Troy" Colgan, of Troy, New York, who had previously fled from two other prisons.

$100 REWARD

For the arrest of each of the following prisoners who escaped from the Ulster County Jail, Sunday, August 22d. Their description is as follows:

JOHN BOYLAN.—About 27 years of age, 5 feet, 7 inches in height, weight about 170 pounds. Is stocky built, smooth, reddish face, short dark hair, and wore black clothes, sack coat, black derby, and comparitively new pair of shoes, size No. 6.

WILLIAM LASHER—About 25 years of age, 5 feet, ten inches in height, weight about 150 pounds. Is slim built, had moustache of a few weeks' growth and dark brown hair. Wore a drab suit of clothes and a brown derby hat, tan colored shoes.

PHILIP SCHANTZ, Sheriff.

KINGSTON, N. Y., August 22, 1897.

An 1897 postcard sent from Sheriff Philip Shantz's office offering a $100 reward for the arrest of John Boylan and William Lasher, who escaped from the Ulster County Jail. *Elizabeth Werlau's collection.*

In 1898, at the age of eighteen, Colgan notoriously escaped from the Elmira Reformatory after single-handedly overcoming four guards. Two years later, he was placed at the Albany Penitentiary, where he used a set of smuggled saws to break through windows in the prison's most secure cell— an inside cell that required Colgan to break through four successive rooms before he was able to cut through a window and lower himself to the ground with the aid of several blankets tied together.

Colgan and another inmate took time planning their leave from Eastern, securing street clothes from the prison's tailor shop and smuggling window sash cords into their cells. Choosing to stay in their cells during a routine Sunday morning chapel service, the two men escaped by climbing to the top of the gallery, changing into street clothes, maneuvering through a small window to the roof and lowering themselves down to the ground nearly sixty feet below with the window sash cords. With most of the guards occupied by chapel service, they were able to "walk leisurely away," which they lost no time doing." The unnamed prisoner was captured that evening in Ellenville, but Colgan—a slightly built man of twenty-three described as having a freckled face, sharp features and "warty moles on his back between the shoulders"—managed to remain on the lam for several months.

The warden's residence in Eastern Reformatory, Napanoch, New York. *Elizabeth Werlau's collection.*

Colgan had a close call the day after his exodus, when he was spotted on Hurley Avenue in Kingston. A group of prison keepers, assigned to search for him in that city, caught up with him. One of the jail staffers was able to fire four shots. A single shot briefly felled Colgan, but he was able to scramble away before the search party gained on him. By a creek near the Ulster and Delaware railroad bridge, the prison crew came upon Colgan's shoes and a "huge knife which he had been carrying." It was a deadly weapon that "had been sharpened on both sides and ground down until it tapered to a point." There was no trace of Colgan, however. It is believed that the man was able to get away on a West Shore freight train headed to New York City. Several months later, he was captured there on Bleecker and Sullivan Streets "after a desperate fight." Colgan was returned to Eastern to finish the twenty-one remaining months of his original sentence for armed robbery.

The July 21, 1903 edition of the *Kingston Daily Freeman* was quick to point out some security lapses at Eastern that made Colgan's escape possible:

> *Given an unguarded stockade, enclosed by a wooden fence of the barnyard type, constructed with posts and stringers inside, so that a small boy could*

easily scale it, ungrated windows in the roof, with a saw horse placed conveniently underneath, and lots of clothesline handy by, and "outside clothes" in the tailor shop to be smuggled out and concealed at will, it is only to be wondered at that escapes are not of daily occurrence. Evidently the Napanoch theory is to treat the convicts so well that they will not care to leave their happy home.

Security was tightened after the Colgan incident, but as the reformatory offered many opportunities for prisoners to work as trustees, the chance to escape continued to prove tempting to many. As one sergeant, by the name of Bailey, remarked to a *Kingston Daily Freeman* reporter in the summer of 1904, "This time of year is a hard one for us. All the men work outside and we have to be very careful about them. Then, too, the mountains look very inviting, to men kept in as they are."

Just as tempting as the mountains were to inmates who wanted to break free, the nearby railroad station and train tracks offered prisoners a way to sneak passage to a distant place. While strategizing their escapes, most inmates only got as far as planning to head for one of these targets, which aided authorities greatly in their recapture. For instance, in 1906, four prisoners by the name of Brandes, Gordon, Burns and La Pratt attempted to escape just after their day's work had ended. Using a secret signal, two of the men ran toward the mountains while the other two fled for the tracks. It took only half an hour for authorities to catch up with them.

As prison breaks became more frequent, a reward of fifty dollars was offered for the return of inmates who had managed to escape. In 1907, prisoner Byron Golby was captured in a nearby cornfield by Napanoch postmaster H.F. Kuhfeldt. Before being caught, Golby had nearly missed being shot at least five times during his six short hours of freedom; the local newspaper reported that "there were over one hundred men and boys after him, as there is a reward of $50 for each capture."

In 1908, two inmates, apparently with bad luck, chose to use the train tracks for their escape route. Unknowingly, they followed the tracks right to the property of Kerhonkson constable Will Geary, who had been unable to sleep that night. He had the uncomfortable feeling "that something was coming this way." One prisoner ran right by Geary, who grabbed him by the arm and, recognizing the prison uniform, ordered him to stop. Geary, who was not armed, threatened to shoot the other inmate if he continued running. The second man stopped in his tracks; neither man resisted Geary as he and his son shackled them and returned them to Napanoch.

"Reformatory", Ellenville, N.y.

Napanoch Prison in Napanoch, New York, just outside Ellenville. *Elizabeth Werlau's collection.*

Perhaps the most inept escape attempt from Eastern came in September 1928, when inmate Stewart Gillett attempted to flee by hiding on a cellblock roof for three days. Imprisoned for his role in a hold-up, Gillett was at first successful in his plan. He eluded searchers, who had been scouring the countryside for him, until he decided to leave the roof of the reformatory. Stewart climbed over a gate and was able to reach the wall surrounding Eastern. Tasting freedom, he jumped from the wall—right into the arms of guard Hubert Roberts, one of several sentries who had been posted along the outside fence.

Gillett's actions, and those of most Eastern inmates, paled in comparison to those of a man by the name of Charles Johnston, who made a name for himself at the Ulster County Jail in 1906. Johnston was so inebriated that he actually tried to break into the new jail, all the while yelling incoherently. He got as far as climbing the fence that encircled it when he was caught by a guard. The *Kingston Daily Freeman* reported that during the following morning, he did not have to worry about busting into jail again because he was now safe and secure, having been given a sixty-day sentence and "a nice ride there in the patrol wagon."

13

MEDICINAL PURPOSES

The Atkins family had a good thing going in the village of New Paltz. Hiram Atkins was a well-known businessman who operated a hotel, owned numerous properties and ran one of the largest distilleries in America during the 1880s. On paper, he was an upstanding citizen and leading capitalist in the village of New Paltz. Despite a lack of schooling in his youth, by his later teens, he had already begun a career as a merchant and was known for doing brisk trade in the New Paltz hamlet of Butterville. His success led to the purchase of an extensive farm in New Paltz, and by 1863, Atkins had established a distillery at 10 Main Street in the village of New Paltz, where, along with the help of his son Henry, he brewed apple brandy that was marketed as "for medicinal purposes."

In reality, Atkins operated an extensive—and illegal—brewing operation that first drew the notice of the New Paltz Town Board in the 1870s. The board passed a resolution in October 1872 to prosecute Atkins for operating and selling liquor without a license. Atkins did have approval for brewing a certain amount of brandy and thus readily paid fees required for stamps that would mark each barrel, showing that he had paid the necessary taxes, which amounted to nearly seventy cents per gallon. But rumors persisted, most likely started by some of his competitors, that Atkins was brewing and storing more than he was legally permitted.

For the most part, Atkins kept a low profile. He managed his hotel and spent a great deal of time expanding his farm. Prior to the 1870s, his closest brush with the law had been as a plaintiff in a lawsuit against Abram LeFever in which both men were arguing over who owned a certain locust post. The lawsuit cost both men several hundred dollars in fees, while the value of the post was determined to be worth $2.50.

An 1875 lithograph showing the residence of Hiram Atkins in New Paltz. *Elizabeth Werlau's collection.*

Atkins's distillery began to draw more notice, however, as he started showing a marked interest in local politics. By the 1880s, it was clear that his focus was on the candidates running for the post of town excise commissioner. He threw his full support behind the candidate who supported the licensure of alcoholic beverages.

Around the same time Atkins was backing his candidate, his younger son, Henry, also known as H.H., met a "prepossessing blonde" young woman named Harriet Link. He wooed and wed her within a short period of time. Within a year of their marriage, however, an incident occurred that would change the fortunes of both H.H. and Atkins.

Newspaper accounts of the event vary, but all agree that while attending the Veterans' Association of New Paltz Ball in the winter of 1881, Link made the acquaintance of a young man named Jake Freer. Various accounts indicate that Link snuck Freer into her bedroom on the night of the ball while H.H. was on business in Rondout. Other interpretations indicate that H.H. and Freer both became so drunk at the ball that Freer wound up spending the night and somehow managed to make his way to Link's bedroom in the process. Whatever the case, when H.H. found Freer in Link's room, he flew into a rage and forced his wife out of the house, although he allowed Freer to remain there in order to sleep off his hangover.

By her own admission, Link slipped into a case of temporary insanity "caused by the worry, excitement and disgrace of the suit for divorce" that was proceeding against her in the city of Kingston. Within a month of being removed from her home by H.H., Link regained her senses and sought revenge on her husband. In an interview with a *Kingston Daily Freeman* reporter, Link alleged that her estranged husband and father-in-law had been distilling whiskey for at least eight years—much more than the government-sanctioned amount—and that she had seen them burying barrels on Atkins's farm. On a Tuesday morning in March 1881, when Atkins "stood at the polls soliciting votes for a license Excise Commissioner," federal revenue officers paid a visit to Link's former father-in-law. They confiscated his business and all the machinery and property associated with it.

Evidently, Atkins and H.H. had some inkling of what was to transpire, for when the officers arrived, they found bottles hastily buried and several barrels of whiskey concealed beneath the newly built floor of a henhouse on the property. On March 5, 1881, both Atkins and H.H. were arrested on the charge of "manufacturing illicit whiskey" and held on $1,000 bail. The bail was raised to $20,000 once Hiram's businesses and property holdings were totaled.

Atkins's property, valued between $7,000 and $10,000, was seized by the government, as were $2,500 worth of distilled spirits and cider. In addition to the whiskey discovered in the hennery, interviews conducted with local farmers, who had brought their apples to Atkins in the past, turned up seventeen barrels of unstamped applejack that Atkins had previously stored in their cellars. Each farmer claimed that he thought he was storing cider or had taken barrels of cider in return for payment of various services. Many also claimed that Atkins's health had been poor, rendering him unable to serve as the head of a large illegal brewing operation.

One farmer, who unknowingly agreed to store cider for Atkins, apparently learned what was really in the barrels after his wife complained of the smell of alcohol near the stored containers. He told authorities that upon opening one of the casks, he discovered that it contained apple-brandy. He then pried all of the barrels open and emptied them into the ground.

Additional evidence against Atkins was found on the Springtown farm of Atkins's nephew, Lewis Atkins. At that location, federal agents found trenches from which four barrels of whiskey had apparently been freshly removed. Atkins's nephew was later arrested on the charge of perjury for statements made to the agents in his uncle's defense.

Several prominent New Paltz businessmen raised the necessary funds to bail Atkins and H.H. out of the New York City jail where they had been

New Paltz businessman, and alleged bootlegger, Hiram Atkins. *Elizabeth Werlau's collection.*

detained for several days. Despite local support for Atkins and his son, however, their trial was swift, and a verdict was made against their favor. The United States government determined that Atkins and H.H. had cheated the government by at least $2,000 in revenue, just in the present year's brewing. Because they had been distillers for a while, it was determined that they had been conducting illegal operations for quite some time.

By the fall of 1881, the jury supported the government, allowing it to retain the land and machinery seized in the raid earlier that year, valued at $17,000. The government was actually aided by Hiram, who refused to speak about his case to reporters. He offered very little information in his own defense, perhaps to protect his extensive network of customers.

The result of the trial did little to diminish the reputations of the two men, but it did bring about an end to the Atkins cider business. Atkins focused his attentions on grape cultivation and other farm matters, but the stress of the trial and loss of revenue took its toll on his already frail health. He died in 1883, at the age of sixty-three, and was laid to rest in the New Paltz Rural Cemetery. A brief biography was published in the 1881 *History of Ulster County, New York*, which glossed over Atkins's most recent brush with the law and served to protest his innocence as he refused to do when alive: "Prompt and honorable in all of his business transactions, a kind and obliging neighbor, liberal to the poor, he has always commanded the good will and esteem of the community in which he lived."

14
SLEUTHETTES

When combing through many of the newspapers in Ulster County's long history, it was a surprise to discover that not only did the county possess some of the best sheriffs and detectives but it also contained a rarity: "lady detectives." The papers, as well as county citizens, were captivated with great zeal by this new breed of investigators. One of the more well known of the "Lady Sleuths" was Miss Alice Heath. However, this "sleuthette" was not who she appeared to be, as two men found out way too late.

Heath resided in New York City. One day, she decided she would journey roughly sixty miles up the Hudson River to the city of Newburgh. As she made her way north on the train, she chatted amicably with people she met along the way, explaining to anyone who might listen that she was a detective on the trail of a notorious individual. When people inquired about how she found herself in this line of work, she replied that her father owned a detective agency. Heath bathed in all the attention people on the train lavished upon her. Passengers found her intriguing because, in 1909, a female detective was quite uncommon. Passengers begged and even tried to cajole her into giving them even the tiniest hint about the quarry she was after; in doing so, she revealed that it might compromise the case.

Once Heath arrived in Newburgh, the "sleuthette" checked into the Palatin Hotel, one of the most upscale establishments in the city. After having her bags placed in her room, Heath inquired about where to rent a motorcar, as she needed to go to Kingston in Ulster County. She was directed to Hornbeck's Garage situated on Second Street. When she

Palatine Hotel. *A.J. Schenkman's collection.*

arrived, the proprietor of the shop apologized that at the moment he did not have a car to rent. However, he did know of another local garage, which was a short distance away, where he was sure they'd have a car for her. Mr. Hornbeck directed her to the Empire Garage owned by two men named Mr. Clapper and Mr. Sloan.

Hornbeck was correct—the partners did have a vehicle available to rent. They explained the terms of the rental to Heath, including that her usage of the car would cost fifty-five dollars. She proclaimed that money was not a problem for her, but she would need a driver because she did not know how to operate these relatively new machines. Perhaps taken with her beauty, Sloan decided that he was up for the task. He offered to accompany Heath the next day.

There was just one issue that vexed Sloan: he needed to know why Heath needed to travel all the way to Kingston. Heath was reluctant to confide in Sloan, but after assurances that he could keep a secret, she explained that she hailed from New York City, where her father owned a detective agency. A man in the city had hired her to trail his wife because he was convinced that she was having an affair. It appears he was correct and that his wife and her lover were in Kingston.

The following morning, Sloan chaperoned the woman as he had promised. They motored for the better part of the day and finally approached Kingston. Once there, Heath instructed Sloan to drop her off at a specified hotel. The name of the hotel is unfortunately lost to time. Heath's plan was to meet with the chief of police to share with him what she had discovered, but after a bit of thinking, she decided that it might be best to simply call him. By this time, Sloan was becoming suspicious of the woman's actions, and her stories were beginning to make him nervous. Why would she need to alert the chief of police of Kingston of her research? Sloan told Clapper, who was back at the shop, that he felt something was not quite right about this woman. He decided that when he next saw Heath, he would present her with a bill so that he could return to Newburgh.

When Heath received an invoice for services rendered by Sloan to her thus far, which included the fifty-five-dollar rental car fee, she laughed. She assured the nervous driver that he need not worry. She was planning on returning to Newburgh very soon, as she had instructed her father to meet her at the Palatine. Heath promised Sloan that her father would settle up her bills. Sloan still felt uneasy about how Heath convinced him to wait for his money. As he parted ways with her, something still did not sit right with him; trusting his gut, he doubled back to the hotel only to find out that Heath had checked out. She then reappeared and assured Sloan that she had checked out because she needed him to drive her to the train station at Newburgh.

Instead of heading to the train station, Sloan drove to his garage. Once there, with Heath looking a little nervous, the partners pushed for their payment, which was now in excess of fifty-five dollars. Heath persisted that she needed to meet with her father so that he could settle matters, as she did not have cash with which to pay them. Clapper was at his wit's end and called the police on Heath. He was told that this was not their problem.

While the two men decided their next of course of action, Heath made an escape. Once the pair, who had been deep in thought, realized that Heath had absconded, they searched all over for her, but it was too late. "Detective" Heath was already en route to New York City after enjoying a wonderful drive in the country at Sloan and Clapper's expense.

Apparently, Heath was not the only "sleuthette." There was another female detective with whom Ulster County became enamored during the same time period. The newspapers joked that she was so adept at her trade that she might possibly be the widow of the one and only Sherlock Holmes, a reference to the dime novels of the period. The papers did not divulge for whom she was working, but it was apparent that she was building a case against some local dentists. They were engaging in an extracurricular activity that was taboo in the early part of the century.

One of the more famous dime novel characters during this period was Nick Carter. It appears from a *Washington Post* article that writers were trying to create female detectives with their famous husbands' last names, so the newspapers called this latest sleuthette Mrs. Nick Carter. Newspapers described her as stunningly beautiful. Her attractiveness held only more allure to newspaper readers. Their imaginations went wild when they heard, on good authority, that some dentists in Ulster County in 1909 were "alleged to be running moonshine tooth-yanking plants" in violation of the Pure Food and Drug Law. Carter, though it is not clear if this was her actual name, was determined to uncover this operation. Possibly working for the state or federal government, the female detective made Kingston uneasy as she not only targeted the dentists but also local grocers, asking the proprietors of the stores to examine their stock. After not finding what she was looking for, Carter left the city—much to the relief of Kingston residents.

15
WOMEN'S WORK

The hamlet of Clintondale lies partially within the town of Plattekill and partially within the town of Lloyd. For much of their history, the boundary between the two towns has meant little, as services such as fire protection and the education of children have been amicably shared between them. During one point in the early 1900s, however, an issue arose that fiercely divided residents along the border of the two southern Ulster County towns. Plattekill had been a dry town for decades, and aside from the wines and ciders made by local farmers, the sale and distribution of alcohol was illegal. Lloyd permitted such sales, although in the rural region near Clintondale, there were few establishments that offered such temptations. With a history rooted in Quaker values and the strong presence of the Clintondale Woman's Christian Temperance Union (WCTU) in the area, the matter of alcohol sales was merely a subject for debate in Clintondale, until John Auchmoody of Ohioville made the decision to open a hotel in the hamlet with every intention of establishing a saloon under its roof.

The WCTU had long found that its efforts were supported in Plattekill, a no-license town where sales and distribution of liquor were not permitted. It focused much of its energy on towns such as Lloyd, where alcohol sales were legal, and on Ulster County temperance activities in general. Auchmoody's purchase of the former "Pinkham lot" in March 1902 hardly seemed a cause for concern, until he announced that he would be applying for a liquor license for his new hotel, just down the street from the Clintondale Post Office.

Confiscated alcohol—the temperance movement sought to convince people to give up drinking. *Courtesy of the Library of Congress.*

The heart of the issue was the location of Auchmoody's hotel. Situated in the town of Lloyd, along what is present-day South Street, the property was within walking distance of the village of Clintondale and situated on the main road through the hamlet. In the minds of the WCTU members, the business could prove tempting to local residents, business owners and their customers and, worst of all, students of the nearby school.

The WCTU, led by Hulda Sutton (the undertaker's wife), Olive Ryon (the Quaker minister's wife and a minister herself) and Kate Covert worried that after more than thirty years as a dry town, Plattekill residents might be unduly influenced and become lax in enforcing their own laws. It did not take long for the determined women of the WCTU to put other projects on hold and turn all their attention to stopping Auchmoody from moving forward. An emergency meeting was called for the purpose of brainstorming ideas. A plan was born when member Fannie Hull stepped forward to offer the use of some property she owned, which just happened to be the lot adjoining Auchmoody's. Fully dedicated to the cause, Hull offered the use of her land to the organization for whatever purpose they decided.

The women, "all of whom thought they were doing their Christian duty," while "endeavoring to crush out the hotel," were well aware of existing

Ulster County legislation that would greatly aid their case. Within towns that allowed the sale of alcoholic beverages, the laws on the books required the approval of all residents living within a two-hundred-foot radius of the proposed site of a hotel or a saloon. Hull's offer of her vacant lot meant one thing: the woman had to build a house and find a resident willing to stand up to Auchmoody.

The women began clearing Hull's lot with picks and shovels, but many found that the tools were too heavy for them to work with efficiently. On the suggestion of a member, they instead turned to light garden tools and were able to accomplish the task they set about to do. Their choice of tools caught the attention of passersby, and the story of their work spread quickly. Within a week, national newspapers were reporting on the efforts of the Clintondale women, who had turned their "sewing circle" into a "council of war."

Once a large enough area was cleared, the same women began the job of constructing a small home by organizing a "building bee." A reporter for a local newspaper commented on their efforts:

> *Tireless energy and no particular knowledge of carpentry were the requisites…they dug ditches, hauled stones over while the foundation was being built, and in various ways assisted with their presence and their efforts to erect the house so much needed, while their patient husbands were at home mending stockings, doing the cooking and singing nursery rhymes to their children who needed a mother's attention.*

Within a short time, a "simple hut," stood just one hundred feet from Auchmoody's hotel, where just a week before, a vacant and overgrown lot had existed.

The next step was securing a tenant. The women advertised far and wide, making their intentions to use the house as a deterrent to Auchmoody's business well known. In January 1903, the *Christian Nation* newspaper advertised that "if a tenant cannot be secured, one of the women will act as tenant and thus exclude the saloon." A tenant was soon found for the new home, one who refused consent for the new hotel. Confident that the WCTU house was not a true residence, Auchmoody went ahead with his plans and opened his hotel. At the same time, he applied for and was granted a liquor tax certificate "to traffic in liquors at a hotel in Clintondale, in the County of Ulster," after stating on the record that no residences existed within two hundred feet of his property. Abundant vineyards in both Plattekill and Lloyd made locally distilled wine cheap

Police officers pouring illegal alcohol down the sewer. The temperance movement would be instrumental in bringing about the Eighteenth Amendment to the Constitution. *Courtesy of the Library of Congress.*

and available, and with his new license, Auchmoody immediately began to buy alcohol from local farmers.

The WCTU sought help from Ryon's husband, Fred, who was the minister of the Clintondale Friends Meeting. The Ryons, who were boarding with Hull, were staunch believers in temperance. Ryon readily joined the WCTU when she moved to Clintondale with her husband in an effort to promote the cause. The young couple appealed the county's decision to grant Auchmoody a license and sought to have his liquor license annulled.

In their appeal, the Ryons, represented by Ulster County district attorney Charles F. Cantine, argued that Auchmoody's establishment did not have the required number of rooms dictated by county code to be considered a hotel. In addition, they claimed that his guest register, also required by code, was simply a slip of paper on which two of Auchmoody's friends had signed their names. They also testified that none of the rooms in the building had the "required number of cubic feet of space" and that Auchmoody was running the establishment as a saloon rather than a hotel, which was a violation of his license. It was found that Auchmoody had covered the windows of one room completely with heavy screens and shades; it was this room from which he had been selling alcohol to local residents. The WCTU scored a victory when Auchmoody's license was revoked for not securing the consent of the surrounding property owners. Auchmoody claimed that he did not need the approval of the residents in the new house because it was not a legitimate dwelling; rather, it was a "shack" constructed "out of spite."

Kingston judge John Van Etten felt otherwise and ruled that whatever motivated the building of the home was irrelevant and that the "Spite House," as it came to be called, was a legitimate residence. Like Ryon, the judge believed that Auchmoody's hotel was a poor cover for a saloon. The case moved to the New York State Supreme Court in Albany, where it was decided that liquor tax certificate Number 30,326 would be revoked on the grounds that Auchmoody had made false statements on his application when he stated that there were no residences within two hundred feet of his hotel.

The decision did not sit well with Auchmoody's supporters, and the fight took a bitter turn. The Spite House was burned to the ground in 1903 by unknown arsonists during a brief period of vacancy. Ryon wryly wrote of the incident that "the wind being favorable, no damage was done to the liquor selling establishment." The arsonists were not satisfied with their work, however, and within weeks set fire to the home shared by Hull and the Ryons. Luckily, the occupants discovered the fire in time and were able to put it out before much damage was done.

Auchmoody and his supporters were not done with the WCTU or the minister who was backing them. A second attempt was made, in May 1903, to burn down the minister's house, when an unknown man doused the front porch in oil and set it on fire. A bright light outside caught Ryon's attention, and he fired off several shots at a man fleeing from the property. Ryon and Hull were able to stop the fire, thanks to the full tubs of water they had been storing in the kitchen after the first blaze. A third attempt to set fire to the place was made shortly after. Perhaps frustrated by their thwarted efforts to chase the Ryons out of their home, the criminals began sending messages to Olive Ryon, threatening that she would "be made the sorriest woman that ever was."

Fred Ryon kept a written record of the events taking place within the town at this time and noted that "after the liquor license was revoked by the County Judge, the saloonist immediately secured a license in his wife's name for the carrying on of the same unlawful business in the same place. Thus the business was protected by the liquor license system of the great

Clintondale Friends minister Fred Ryon, who was run out of town by arsonists for his temperance efforts. *Courtesy of Shirley Anson.*

State of New York." In late 1903, Auchmoody had won the next round in his struggle with the WCTU. Like her husband had done the first time, Elizabeth Auchmoody stated in her papers that there was no residence within two hundred feet of the hotel. The county granted her a hotel license on the condition that the shaded rooms mentioned in the earlier appeal were updated to fit the standards of a hotel.

The Ryons vowed to keep up the fight but eventually lost the insurance on the house they shared with Hull because of the ongoing attacks on their home and property. Congregants would take the family in for a night or two, but no one was willing to have the Ryons stay with them for an extended period, owing to the fear of fire.

Forced to consider their own safety, Fred Ryon asked members of the Friends Meeting to research the possibility of building a parsonage that would offer more protection for his family. The congregation stood firmly behind the Ryons and raised the needed funds to construct a new parsonage next to the meetinghouse on Crescent Avenue. The fight had taken a toll on the Ryons, however, who were worn down by "the strain and sleepless nights through which they had lived."

J. Lindley Spicer, yearly meeting superintendent of the Friends group, met with the Ryons and encouraged them to leave for another town where they would be safe and could focus on their work. After taking his advice into consideration, the Ryons made a decision in the spring of 1904 to move to another congregation upstate. A 1939 history of the Clintondale Friends Meeting reports that "they suffered many hardships and much inconvenience as well as actual threats upon their lives, this by the liquor forces because of their dedicated stand."

The members of the Clintondale WCTU continued their protest of Auchmoody's saloon, but eventually, the publicity surrounding the events died down, and the Auchmoody hotel operated legitimately. It was later converted into a residence, which still stands today. The attention brought about by the lengthy fight in the early 1900s shed light on the cause of temperance; as a result, membership rolls swelled for the Clintondale WCTU just in time for the women to focus their efforts on the broader issue of Prohibition. As for the Ryons, while they returned to the town of Plattekill from time to time, they eventually devoted their efforts to the welcoming residents of Cayuga County, New York, where they were finally free from what Ryon's husband would later write of as the "Reign of Terror" that marked their ministry in Ulster County.

16

A COWBOY IN OLD ULSTER COUNTY

When most people think of the fieldstone house known as Washington's Headquarters, located in the city of Newburgh, they think first of the ardent patriot Colonel Jonathan Hasbrouck and later of the commander-in-chief of the Continental army, General George Washington. Washington utilized Hasbrouck's home as his headquarters from 1782 to 1783. Numerous other high-ranking officials and well-known figures in the Continental army also stayed there, including Baron Von Stueben. What the home is not associated with are the crimes of Hasbrouck's son Cornelius, who supposedly acted out against the country.

In July 1780, when Hasbrouck passed away due to ill health, Newburgh had become quite a busy place. This especially held true along the waterfront. The Hasbroucks subsequently profited greatly from the Continental army using Newburgh, then a part of Ulster County, as a depot and shipping point for supplies. The Hasbroucks' vast meadows were also utilized by the army's livestock. In addition, the significance of the area made the mills that Hasbrouck passed along to his sons very valuable.

Newburgh's importance as a storage point continued to increase; this sometimes brought the military into direct conflict with the populace. One such example was Lieutenant Sullivan, of the Light Dragoons, placing his horses in the pasture of Elnathan Foster. A court case ensued, and Foster successfully attained an order for Sullivan to remove the horses, as they were illegally placed on his property. Sullivan refused to remove the horses and even threatened to physically assault anyone who attempted to do so. This

Front door of the Hasbrouck House. *Courtesy of the Library of Congress.*

left a bad taste in the mouths of citizens, including a despondent Cornelius, who was at Weygant's Tavern where court was held.

Later in the same year that Hasbrouck passed away, his son became increasingly agitated about the abundance of oxen and cows that were being kept on his property. According to the testimony of John Simpson and John Stillwell, the army, as part of an agreement, kept livestock in the pastures of Cornelius. Though the cattle were not placed there against his will, as in Foster's case, it had been a long time since the army compensated him for housing the animals or the damage they caused to both fencing and fields.

Part of Cornelius's agreement with the army was that he had to accommodate the Continental army drover when he wasn't staying with Henry Smith, a neighbor. The drover watched over the cattle and moved them between pastures. Cornelius became increasingly irate at his treatment by the army, voicing his anger to both Stillwell and Simpson. He was tired of waiting for the money that was owed to him. Cornelius then made a fateful choice that would cost him dearly and affect the rest of his life. He paced the floorboards of his father's fieldstone home as he decided to appropriate some army cattle as payment for services rendered.

Stillwell, a local innkeeper and butcher for the Continental army, was approached by Cornelius with a complaint about an ox that kept escaping from his pasture. He asked Stillwell to kill the ox; he could then either keep the meat as payment or Cornelius would pay him for slaying and butchering the animal. Stillwell looked over the ox and quickly realized that this was no ordinary animal; it was the property of the Continental army. A brand indicating this clearly appeared on the animal's horn. After a brief discussion, Stillwell told Cornelius that if he produced the appropriate legal paperwork, he would gladly slaughter the animal; otherwise, there would be no deal.

Cornelius was persistent and would not take no for an answer. He again approached Stillwell. This time, he convinced Stillwell that they could make a lot of money stealing some of the army's livestock. If they decided to go this route, they would have to make a move immediately. For reasons only known to Stillwell, he went along with the scheme and enlisted the help of Simpson, to whom Cornelius had recently sold some land.

The plan would be executed at night when it was believed the drover would be sound asleep. Cornelius would send a slave to act on his behalf while he remained at home. This annoyed his partners in crime. They wanted Cornelius involved, as they started to wonder if he was setting them up.

Cornelius maintained that he would remain in his home during the scheme. Despite this, the other two men journeyed over to his house and knocked on the door. They noticed that all the lights were out. After repeated attempts to rouse someone, no one came to the door, and they returned to the gate where the oxen were kept. Simpson and Stillwell "threw down the fence" and turned out six head of cattle and "six other head followed."

They drove the cattle as far as the home of Stillwell, who became nervous after realizing what he had done. Stillwell instructed Simpson to lead the cattle into the pasture of Benjamin Smith. Cornelius appeared at Stillwell's house the next day; Stillwell confessed that he wanted nothing to do with the crime, especially due to the obvious brands on the animals' horns. Cornelius believed that they could be easily removed and was not worried.

Later, Cornelius claimed that he came upon two oxen that appeared not to be branded. He again approached Stillwell to see if he wanted to profit from peddling these animals; Stillwell promptly refused a second time. This was just fine with Cornelius, as he told Simpson to keep the cattle; if no one claimed them, he could sell them. Cornelius planned on making over $1,000, but he eventually settled for a lesser bargain.

In his testimony, Simpson stated that he decided to purchase the cattle from Cornelius. Cornelius promptly told him that if anyone asked where he bought the two animals, he was to implicate the Continental drover. Furthermore, Simpson was to assert that he had been asked for $2,000 for the cattle, but when he questioned the drover about the brands, he dropped the price. Once the story was agreed on, Simpson drove the cattle to Knapp's pasture, where they remained for a number of days. Stillwell appeared a short time after and again became interested in the animals, trading a mare he owned for the duo. If the endeavor had ended there, perhaps the ordeal of Cornelius might have been an easier one. However, seeing that money could be made from these animals, he became greedy.

Cornelius approached Simpson and asked if he'd take in another animal, this time a cow from Cornelius's field by his late father's mill. Like the oxen, this cow belonged to the Continental army. If Simpson agreed to purchase the animal and rid Cornelius of it, he could slaughter it at Stillwell's home, and they could divide it equally. When Simpson became hesitant about the plot, Cornelius told him to call on two family friends, Knapp and Martin Weygant Jr. If he used Cornelius's name, they would be all too glad to assist Simpson.

Simpson soon made his way to both Knapp's and Weygant Jr.'s homes. He explained that he needed their assistance in bringing a cow from the field near Cornelius's mill to Stillwell's for butchering. When the three set out to do so, Knapp and Weygant Jr. balked when they saw the cow grazing in the field. When asked what the problem was, they explained that the cow had a bell around its neck. Simpson looked perplexed until they described to him that a bell often indicated that the animal belonged to someone. They envisioned that it was probably the property of some old man, perhaps his only milk cow. Simpson insisted that the cow belonged to Cornelius, but they would not budge until they were reassured by Cornelius himself that this was not some senior citizen's cow; the animal belonged to him, and it was fine to butcher it.

Instead, Knapp and Weygant Jr. decided to take an ox with the brand C.M. on its rear. When Cornelius caught wind of this, he asked for $700 for the animal, which was eventually given to him. This ox was slaughtered at Stillwell's, and a portion of the meat was given to Knapp and Weygant Jr. for "their troubles."

These criminal activities ultimately ended with Cornelius, Stillwell and Simpson being arrested. The testimonies of Stillwell and Simpson were instrumental in convicting Cornelius. He came to terms with his situation and pleaded guilty to his misdoings, asking only for the mercy of the court, as well as a "clergyman" to pray with him in jail.

Not surprisingly, the harshest punishment was reserved for Cornelius because he was acknowledged as the ringleader in all matters concerning the stolen animals. Once Cornelius confessed and was "indicted, tried [sic] and convicted of being an accessory both before and after the fact in grand larceny of sundry oxen of the goods and chattels of the United States of America," he was branded. It came out in testimony that at least some of the stolen animals might have been delivered to the British; hence, Cornelius could be considered to be a cowboy. ("Cowboy" was a term used during the American Revolution to describe colonial fighters who opposed the movement for independence.)

In a letter dated January 13, 1781, Judge Robert Yates wrote to Governor George Clinton. His correspondence included the sworn testimonies of Stillwell and Simpson. He alerted Clinton that Cornelius had been tried and convicted in the theft of Continental army cattle. Clinton was no doubt made aware of the examinations of Knapp and Weygant Jr. as well. Yates stated "that Congress may upon your Excellency's representation, appoint pursuant to a law of this State a procurator or attorney, for the purpose of commencing suits ags't him" in order to recover damages from Cornelius.

A second letter was penned the next day by the secretary of the New York Assembly, John McKesson, to the New York Delegates of Congress. While recounting the court case in his letter, McKesson stressed his belief that an

Backdoor of the Hasbrouck House. *Courtesy of the Library of Congress.*

example needed to be made of Cornelius under a law enacted by the New York State legislature in 1779, which "enabled the recovery of Continental Demands [*sic*] and punishing the misbehavior of persons in Continental employ." He advised that the case for damages be pursued with great haste because Cornelius's jail sentence would expire in less than two months. Since Cornelius appeared to be a man of financial means, he felt it would be easy to obtain reimbursement. Although Cornelius was not the first individual to steal from the Continental army, it appears that he was one of the more high-profile individuals to be made an example of by use of this law.

Cornelius was released from jail on March 4, 1781. He then returned to his home in Newburgh. It appears that almost eight months after he completed his sentence for stealing cattle, Cornelius was in trouble again for journeying to British-occupied New York City without permission.

After being arrested and jailed yet again, he penned a letter to Clinton begging for his understanding and assuring him that he had no sinister motive. Furthermore, Cornelius requested that he be allowed to return home so that he could salvage his already ruined reputation. The governor seemed to take mercy on Cornelius, possibly based on his knowledge of the Hasbrouck family or his friendship with Cornelius's late father and influential uncle, Abraham Hasbrouck of Kingston.

There is no doubt that Cornelius's neighbors considered his actions to be those of a cowboy or Crown sympathizer. His trip to occupied New York City probably cemented this in their minds. For this reason, he might have been remembered for generations as a Tory. A constant reminder of this to his neighbors was the visible "T" branding he wore that proclaimed he could not be trusted.

Eventually, Cornelius left Newburgh. By 1800, a deed in possession of the Huguenot Historical Society in New Paltz listed him as being "late" of Newburgh. Almost all traces of him disappear until 1818, when he drew up property transfers in the town of Sandwich in Upper Canada for, among other things, lands in Newburgh that he had not previously disposed of while he lived there. We also know that he settled a dispute raging over the will of his late uncle, Cornelius DuBois, which involved his surviving siblings and other relatives. This quarrel, as well as a foreclosure notice, made it into the several newspapers of the time. Cornelius settled matters by selling his lands to a Kingston, New York attorney named John Sudam. He also vested power-of-attorney to Sudam. Once this business was concluded, Cornelius disappeared again. Where he went is still a mystery.

17

OCCUPATIONAL HAZARDS

From the bluestone pits in Hurley, Saugerties and Kingston and the cement factories in Rosendale to the river mills in Wallkill and Esopus and the icehouses along the Hudson River, Ulster County's abundant natural resources have long allowed a variety of industrial opportunities to flourish. While providing income to thousands of employees, the early mills, quarries and factories were often dangerous places to work, and only the toughest stuck it out. Fire was a constant threat, and accidents in factories such as the Nitro Powder Works Company, where nitroglycerin and dynamite were produced, could be deadly for those working in the plants as well as in surrounding communities.

At one point, it was said that quarrymen had the shortest lives of all the industrial workers, for those who were not injured or killed by the large heavy bluestone were subject to chronic lung problems caused by the stone dust. Lead poisoning was another hazard at mills such as the Ulster White Lead Company in the Saugerties hamlet of Glenerie. Edward Poll and Karlyn Knaust Elia, who have chronicled the history of Saugerties, note that the company produced a lead disc that, when combined with a water vinegar solution, caused a corrosive reaction that could later be pulverized for use in paints. The mill had a graphic nickname—"the Slow Kill"—for the health hazards caused by working there for any length of time.

The brickyards along the Hudson were also a dangerous place of employment. They were infamous for their strikes, which the *Kingston Daily Freeman* noted in the early 1900s were becoming "an annual tradition." The brickyards were often cited for violations, including flouting child labor laws and overworking immigrant laborers.

It became routine for law enforcement officials to order saloons along the Kingston waterfront to shut down during strikes for fear that workers would become even more agitated with the addition of alcohol. At times, as many as three hundred men would march from brickyard to brickyard in an effort to garner support for higher wages and better working conditions. The murder of one worker by another was not uncommon, and newspapers were rife with stories of notorious young men, such as "the Baltimore Kid," who had killed a co-worker during a petty argument and fled to anonymity in New York City.

One of the most brutal murders at the brickyards involved the four-year-old son of one of its workers, who was of Italian descent. On a summer morning in 1910, the body of Peter Fabiano of Glasco was found in an outhouse on his family's property. According to an account in the *Kingston Daily Freeman*, the child had been "slashed to ribbons" and was discovered as men made their way to work at a nearby brickyard, where Fabiano's father was also employed.

The coroner determined that Fabiano had been beaten, strangled and then mutilated with a knife. His skull was crushed and his body bore postmortem bruises that were determined to have resulted from the way he was positioned in the outhouse. Fabiano had disappeared a few days earlier, while playing with some friends; his family feared that he had drowned in the Hudson. When authorities failed to locate the boy, his father consulted a fortuneteller, who indicated that Fabiano would return "in a day or two."

When Fabiano's body was discovered, authorities focused in on other Italian workers at the brickyards. They assumed that whoever murdered the boy had returned his body within a two-day timeframe in order to fulfill the fortuneteller's prophesy and keep a "curse" away. On the basis of this hunch, they eventually determined that Vincenzo Caruso and his wife, whose property adjoined the elder Fabiano's land, were responsible for the boy's disappearance. Authorities determined that Caruso and Pietro Ortale, another brickyard worker, had a long-standing grudge against Fabiano's father and sought to get even with him by holding his son for ransom. The fortuneteller's prediction led them to murder young Fabiano rather than risk returning him and having him identify them as criminals. All three were eventually convicted of murder in the first degree.

Despite their proximity to the river, the icehouses along the Hudson River were another industry subject to mayhem, often in the form of fire. Ice harvesting was made possible by long winters and the abundant Hudson River, which would freeze over each winter. Hundreds of Ulster County men worked for ice companies to supplement their seasonal employment in the quarries and brickyards. The work was difficult and required laborers to be ever watchful for danger, both from heavy ice and the often poorly maintained equipment that could easily kill a man unlucky enough to be caught unawares.

The Knickerbocker Ice Company was one of several companies with warehouses along the Hudson, housing thousands of tons of ice that would be transported to New York City by barge when the river was once again navigable. In 1882, the business center of the town of Lloyd was destroyed, along with five Knickerbocker icehouses, when a blaze broke out in a barn near Highland Landing. Dry grass along the riverbank fed the fire, and gusty winds helped spread it, engulfing the Knickerbocker holdings, including four dwellings attached to the icehouses. The cause of that fire was unknown.

In 1915, the Mulford Ice House in Glasco, town of Saugerties, which was another icehouse owned by Knickerbocker, caught fire and was completely destroyed after a night watchman knocked over a kerosene lantern. Given

A carpet mill in Rifton, one of the many mills along the Wallkill River later destroyed by fire. *Elizabeth Werlau's collection.*

the number of employees and often sprawling buildings where a worker could easily be trapped, fire was an ever-present danger in many of these early industries. When combined with gunpowder or dynamite, however, the potential for chaos was increased considerably.

A 1905 explosion in an Esopus dynamite mill could have been disastrous—its far-reaching effects were felt in the city of Kingston, where numerous windows were blown out—but miraculously, the man closest to the blast walked away unscathed. The Esopus hamlet of Mingo Hollow, near Port Ewen, was home to the Nitro Powder Works Company, where employee William Delaney noticed a small fire in the mixing house one August afternoon. Because of the extreme heat in the in the mixing house, where oil and glycerin were carefully combined to form nitroglycerine, the fire was thought to have formed as a result of spontaneous combustion. Delany reacted quickly to the situation. While he was in the process of throwing water from a bucket onto the flames, the nitroglycerine room exploded. This blast caused a crater to form in the ground, leaving behind little trace of the room that had once stood on that spot. The surrounding building was soon engulfed in flames, and employees formed a bucket brigade in a futile attempt to save the attached dynamite storehouse.

Surprisingly, apart from a few bruises from being thrown from the nitroglycerin room during the explosion, Delany was uninjured. Other employees reported being thrown to the ground or having their hats blown from their heads, but they were also relatively unharmed. The only victim was employee George Messinger, who had been working near the mixing room and suffered a broken arm and numerous cuts and bruises.

When the nitroglycerin room exploded, men working outside the building reported seeing "a column of smoke, flame and dust of such intensity that it completely shut out the sunlight for an instant." From the nearby city of Kingston, eyewitnesses described reddish smoke that looked like "a column of blood"; for many, it resembled a volcano.

The sight of such chaos caused the county coroner to procure a special West Shore train to rush to the scene. When he discovered that his services were not necessary, he remained at the site, as he was convinced that at least one of the men on the bucket brigade would have succumbed to the force of the flames. Though the main buildings, including the dynamite storehouse, were a complete loss, the coroner's services were fortunately not needed that day.

Several decades earlier, employees at a town of Shawangunk paper mill along the Wallkill River had not been so lucky, as their workplace was the

112

The banks of the Wallkill River, sometimes the scene of murder and mayhem. *A.J. Schenkman's collection.*

scene of one of the grisliest disasters in Ulster County history. The paper mill was the largest business in the village, employing hundreds of men and women from Ulster and Orange Counties. On a quiet Saturday evening in May 1874, the boiler in the Condit Paper Mill exploded, causing the mill to be "as completely demolished as if blown up with gunpowder." Twenty-three men and women were at work when the defective machinery blew up with a roar that was heard for miles around. The large brick and frame building, as well as surrounding outbuildings, were destroyed, and a piece of the boiler, weighing several tons, was reportedly "hurled far away on to an adjacent hill."

The boiler was considered to be suspect for quite some time; some employees went as far as resigning rather than working any longer in the mill. One employee who left had been a fireman in the mill for many years. He felt that his life would be in jeopardy if he continued working there. The steam pressure in the boiler was reported afterward to have been "100 pounds to the square inch," with strained seams that had been leaking for at least six weeks. The boiler ran twenty-four hours a day, with employees working through the night to keep up with the demand for their paper products. Several months prior, unnamed employees had notified a mill inspector, who was refused admittance by company officials. Mill officials objected to his visit by asserting that their pipes would freeze if they shut the boiler down for an inspection in the middle of winter; they promised to send for the inspector when the weather warmed.

On the morning of the accident, several men had noticed that the boiler was leaking worse than ever and reported the situation to mill superintendent Thomas F. Tranter. Rather than shutting the mill down for the day, Tranter telegraphed the mill owner in New Jersey about the situation. Whether the owner responded is unknown, but the mill remained open.

An Ulster County correspondent for the *New York Times* reported that when the boiler exploded, one man was working by an ash tub and "was smashed down into the tub, and, no doubt, killed instantly." Another man, who had just started on the job the evening before, "was hurled over one hundred feet and came down a shapeless mass." Yet another man was found on a rooftop more than one hundred feet from the mill, nearly decapitated.

Two women, twenty-year-old Mary McLaughlin and eighteen-year-old Eliza Conklin, were sitting on chairs near the boiler. If the explosion did not kill them instantly, the roof that caved in above them and crushed them surely did. McLaughlin's uncle, Charles, later stated that he had resigned two weeks before accident because he felt that the boiler was unsafe and feared for his life. In all, seven men and women were killed, while a number of other men and women were scalded, bruised or suffered broken bones. At least four employees were critically injured.

The justice of the peace brought together a jury within a day, forcing an immediate trial. The jury members were brought to the scene of the explosion and were offered a chance to look at the bodies before they were removed from the site. They did not get a chance to see the remains of Michael Flannigan, the man found on the roof, because his body had not yet been located at the time they were touring the site. In a bizarre motion, the Shawangunk coroner halted Flannigan's funeral procession, several days later, as it was leaving Shawangunk for the interment site in the city of Newburgh. He ordered that the coffin be opened so that jurors could view the condition of the body before allowing the procession to continue on to Newburgh.

The paper factory explosion forced safer working conditions in the Wallkill mills. However, another incident that took place years later at a Wallkill factory proved that no matter what precautions were taken, accidents on the jobsite were always possible. George Halliday was a shoe salesman who had the good fortune to marry into the prominent Borden family of Wallkill. The Bordens were well known for their condensed milk, as well as the innovations they had brought to the hamlet of Wallkill and the greater town of Shawangunk. With the help of his wife, Marion Borden Halliday, the former salesman was named president of the Wallkill Manufacturing Company, also known as the Wallkill Hat Factory, a large industrial complex along the Wallkill River that had been a primary source of industry since its erection in 1876. The company was known for the soft felt men's hats produced there.

Borden Halliday was a prominent woman in Ulster County; she was well known for her philanthropic work in the town of Shawangunk and beyond. She had been instrumental in bringing electricity to the hamlet of Wallkill, not only to power her Borden Home Farm but also to light the streets of the village and modernize the businesses along the Wallkill River, including the Wallkill Manufacturing Company. Halliday, on the other hand, was not so successful in his business dealings and had experienced a number of financial troubles by the 1920s. The couple had long been estranged when he met a tragic fate at the Hat Factory.

On the evening of September 1929, a Wallkill Hat Factory employee, William Wastpahl, was the lone witness to an accident. He claimed that Halliday was walking outside of the building when he noticed a wire hanging near the door. Standing on damp ground, Halliday supposedly grasped

The Wallkill Hat Shop, where company president George Halliday was accidently electrocuted. Later known as the Wallkill Dyeing and Finishing Company, the building was destroyed by fire in 1971. *Elizabeth Werlau's collection.*

the wire, and 2,300 volts of electricity passed through his body, killing him instantly. Three doctors worked on him for more than two hours with the help of a machine donated by Central Hudson Gas and Electric Company "to help restore respiration and heart function."

The case was quickly deemed an accident. It came as a surprise to many that very little was known about Halliday, despite the fact that he had lived in the hamlet for many years and was married to such a renowned woman. Borden Halliday held a simple service for him on the Bordens' farm, and he was quietly buried in Dutchess County, where he was born. After his burial, the investigation into the accident was considered to be wrapped up.

Borden employees passed on a story, however, that might or might not have been born in truth. On the night of his accident, Halliday was preparing for dinner with friends, a long-standing appointment that he never missed. Supposedly, he was called from his meal by unknown men in dark suits, and he never returned. The appearance of the men, while apparently never investigated, was only supported by the employees' knowledge of one personality trait of their former employer. Halliday, it was said, was terrified of electricity and would never willingly go near the power supplies of his own factory.

BIBLIOGRAPHY

Books and Journals

Anson, Shirley V., and Laura M. Jenkins. *Quaker History and Genealogy of the Marlborough Monthly Meeting, Ulster County, N.Y., 1804–1900.* Baltimore, MD: Gateway Press, 1980.

Branson, B. Russell. *Clintondale Friends Meeting: In Celebration of the 50th Anniversary of the Building of the Present Meeting House.* Clintondale, NY: Clintondale Friends Meeting, 1939.

Hine, Charles Gilbert. *History and Legend: Fact, Fancy and Romance of the Old Mine Road, Kingston.* Rutgers, NJ: Rutgers University Press, 1963.

Loftin, A.J. "The Ashokan Reservoir: The Creation of the Ashokan Reservoir Changed the Catskills Forever." *Hudson Valley Magazine* (August 2008).

Poll, Edward, and Karlyn Knaust Elia. *Images of America: Saugerties.* Charleston, SC: Arcadia Publishing, 1997.

Schenkman, Adam J. "Cornelius Hasbrouck: The Prodigal Son." *Orange County Historical Society* 40 (November 1, 2011).

Sylvester, Nathaniel Bartlett. *History of Ulster County, New York: With Illustrations and Biographical Sketches of Its Prominent Men and Pioneers.* Woodstock, NY: Overlook Press, 1977.

Wadlin, Beatrice Hasbrouck, and Warren G. Sherwood. *Times and Tales of Town of Lloyd: Including a Restatement of Warren Sherwood's History of the Town of Lloyd.* Highland, NY: privately published, 1974.

Wick, Karl R., and Susan B. Wick. *Images of America: Esopus.* Charleston, SC: Arcadia Publishing, 2003.

NEWSPAPERS AND PERIODICALS

Albany Evening Times. "New York State News." November 13, 1871.

Buffalo New York Daily Courier. "A Deaf and Dumb Murderer." October 13, 1870.

———. "The Ulster County Horror." February 22, 1870.

Christian Nation. "Notes." January 1, 1902.

DeRuyter New York Gleaner. "County and Vicinity." November 20, 1913.

Hudson New York Evening Register. "Horrible Tragedy." February 16, 1870.

Ithaca New York Daily. "Conscience Stricken Confesses Old Murder." March 10, 1913.

Kingston Daily Freeman. "Action Against Seydel." December 22, 1910.

———. "Another Arrest in Fabiano Case." September 5, 1910.

———. "Atkins' Distillery: What Mrs. Harriet O. Atkins Has to Say about It." March 4, 1881.

———. "Attempted Murder." January 9, 1884.

———. "Bad Bill Again Asks Pardon." December 31, 1927.

———. "Bad Bill Denies His Guilt." November 2, 1925.

———. "Bad Bill Escapes Prison." October 4, 1919.

———. "Bad Bill Held for Grand Jury." August 10, 1922.

———. "Bad Bill in Trouble Again." May 1, 1918.

———. "Bad Bill Monroe Goes to Murder Trial." October 29, 1923.

———. "Barrett Held for Grand Jury." December 9, 1924.

———. "Bill on the War Path." November 18, 1916.

———. "Brooks Relatives Claim Property." July 20 1909.

———. "Brown Belonged to Eastman Gang." March 13, 1909.

———. "Brown Butted in on Crap Game." March 17, 1909.

———. "Brown Didn't Turn Red When Angry." March 17, 1909.

———. "Brown Wants Liberty." October 4, 1909.

———. "Brown Will Be Sentenced Monday." March 19, 1909.

———. "Brutal Fight Down Town." May 18, 1909.

———. "Brutal Murder Near Highland." July 15 1909.

———. "Case Against Seydel Finished." December 16, 1910.

———. "Clemente Demaron Killed by Seydel." July 25 1910.

———. "Clintondale Fight Renewed." March 17, 1909.

———. "Clintondale Hotel Case before Appellate Division." May 23, 1903.

———. "Clintondale Man Shoots Himself." November 25, 1907.

———. "Colgan Captured in New York City." November 14, 1903.

———. "Colgan Seen in Kingston." July 22, 1903.

———. "Constable Caught Them." June 17, 1908.

———. "The County's Insane." October 15, 1880.

———. "Demented Man May Be Cooley." July 24 1909.

———. "Did Demaron Have a Rock in Hand?" December 17, 1910.

———. "Escaped from Reformatory." July 14, 1904.

———. "Esopus Tragedy Recalled." July 14, 1920.

———. "Explosion of the Mixing House," August 3, 1905.

———. "Festivities at Hannah's." March 23, 1908.

———. "Firebugs at Work!" May 14, 1903.

———. "Foth May Know of Brooks Murder." July 26 1909.

———. "Four Men Made a Dash for Liberty." October 10, 1906.

———. "Four Sydell Jurors the First Day." December 13, 1910.

———. "Had Been Dead Only 24 Hours." August 25, 1910.

———. "Hannah Can Celebrate." April 22, 1908.

———. "Hannah Has Retired." December 2, 1907.

———. "Hannah Markle Sells Out." September 11, 1908.

———. "Hannah's Bail Is Ready." April 21, 1908.

———. "History of the Year." January 1, 1908.

———. "How They Got Away." July 21, 1903.

———. "Italians in Mass Scattered." July 26 1910.

———. "Jail Lock Picked with Broom Handle." July 23, 1908.

———. "Jaw Broken at Hannah Markle's." April 21, 1908.

———. "John Colley Wanted for Brooks Murder." July 21, 1909.

———. "John Rosso Vindicated." December 6, 1907.

———. "Killing of Demaron Fully Described." December 15, 1910.

———. "Life Convict Accuses Another." November 10, 1923.

———. "Local Death Record." June 5, 1920.

———. "Mangled Body of Child Found." August 24, 1910.

———. "Many Matters in Surrogate's Court." January 14, 1908.

———. "The Markle Saloon." December 4, 1907.

———. "Matters Before the Surrogate." April 24, 1916.

———. "Monroe and Nephew Captured." August 2, 1923.

———. "Monroe Gets Twenty Years." November 1, 1923.

———. "Monroe Held for Grand Jury." August 4, 1923.

———. "Moonshining at New Paltz." March 7, 1881.

———. "Mrs. Seydel Begged Him Not to Shoot." July 27, 1910.

———. "Mrs. Seydel Cried "Shoot!" August 6, 1910.

———. "Mrs. Seydel Tells of the Shooting." December 17. 1910.

———. "Negro Murder Case. " December 30, 1908.

———. "Piano Player Dropped Dead." May 2, 1907.

———. "Prisoner Found in Corn Stack." November 21, 1907.

———. "Report of County Treasurer." November 18, 1874.

———. "Reward Offered for Murderer." July 16 1909.

———. "Schmidle is Dead." November 26 1907.

———. "Seek Bad Bill in Murder Case." July 31, 1923.

———. "Seydel Acquitted of Murder." December 19, 1910.

———." Seydel at Church." December 19, 1910.

———. "Seydel Defense Opened to Jury." December 16, 1910.

———. "Seydel in Town." July 10, 1911.

———. "Seydel Murder Trial." December 12, 1910.

———. "Seydel's Fate in the Hands of Jurors." December 17, 1910.

———. "Sheldon's Body Identified." May 3, 1907.

———. "Sheriff Shultis Gets His Men." December 29, 1916.

———. "Suspect Discharged." July 20, 1909.

———. "This Tramp's Name was Dennis." July 26, 1909.

———. "Three Prisoners Break Out of Jail." July 21, 1908.

———. "Trespass an Excuse for the Shooting." December 15, 1910.

———. "Tried to Break Out of Jail." June 30, 1903.

———. "Tried to Climb Jail Fence." November 13, 1906.

———. "Twenty and Ten Years Ago." May 19, 1906.

———. "Twenty and Ten Years Ago." August 21, 1928.

———. "Twenty Years Ago Today." August 21, 1928.

———. "Ulster Park." June 6, 1908.

———. "Wayward Girl Weary of Life." July 3, 1908.

———. "Zoda Case Adjourned." December 2, 1907.

Middletown Daily Argus. "Prisoners Escape." August 23, 1897.

Middletown Daily Times-Press. "Bad Bill Plans Home in Jersey." July 1, 1915.

Middletown Times Herald. "Twenty-five Years Ago Today." November 10, 1933.

Middletown Times-Press. "Bad Bill Gets Shot by a Guard." April 19, 1911.

———. "Bad Bill Given Five Years." June 30, 1915.

———. "Bad Bill Monroe Is Sent to Sing-Sing for 3 Years." June 10, 1918.

———. "Man Who Saved Guard from Bill Is Pardoned." December 13, 1911.

———. "Pierce Bedford Is Given Jail Term." April 23, 1918.

Newburgh Evening News. "Clintondale Case: Ulster County Temperance People's Fight Against a Saloon." September 9, 1902.

———. "Fire Destroys Wallkill Landmark." November 4, 1971.

New Paltz Independent. "Court Proceedings." October 13, 1870.

———. "A Letter…" November 26, 1874

———. "Levi Bodine." October 27, 1870.

———. "The Mother of Levi Bodine." April 28, 1870.

———. "The Murder-Daniel Hasbrouck." February 21, 1870.

———. "We Publish Below the Balance of Court Proceedings." January 26, 1871.

New Paltz Times. "The Murder of Daniel A. Hasbrouck." January 26, 1871.

———. "Murderous Assault." February 17, 1870.

New York Evening Post. "A Convict Hard to Keep." November 13, 1903.

New York Herald. "The Bodine Murder Trial." October 10, 1870.

———. "Obituary." November 6, 1886.

New York Times. "City and Suburban News." November 20, 1881.

———. "Convict Stabs Guard." June 24, 1912.

———. "He Dies From His Wounds." January 13, 1884.

———. "How Seydel Shot Dameron."July 27, 1910.

———. "A Husband Seeking Divorce." February 4, 1881.

———. "Illicit Distillers Arrested." March 6, 1881.

———. "Italians Defend Demaron." July 26, 1910.

———. "It Is Murder." Thursday," July 15, 1909.

———. "Jumps into Guard's Arms." September 3, 1928.

———. "Kingston's Murder Trial." November 26, 1885.

———. "A Large Distillery Seized." March 4, 1881.

———. "Likely to Prove a Murder: Seeking for Charles Crosby, the Assailant of Edwin Kelland" January 11,1884.

———. "Maintains His Right to Kill Trespasser. "December 15, 1910.

———. "Mr. Kelland's Murderer: A Youth Who Has Been Ruined by Dime Novel Reading." January 16, 1884

———. "A Murderer Arrested, The Crime with which Louis Is Charged." July 3, 1884.

———. "Plotted Against Saloon." April 7, 1902.

———. "Searching for a Boy Murderer." April 5, 1884.

———. "Three Prisoners Escape." August 23, 1897.

———. "Willett in Kingston Jail." July 4, 1884.

———. "Willett to be Hanged." December 5, 1884.

New York Tribune. "Capital Punishment." May 6, 1871.

———. "The Poughkeepsie Murder." October 11, 1870

Orange County Independent. "Touching Wire Is Fatal to Wallkill Man." September 19, 1929.

Orange County Times-Press. "Meyer in Trouble over a Woman." May 3, 1918.

———. "Wm. M. Leonard G.O.P. Candidate for Sheriff Here." November 5, 1918.

Oswego Morning Express. "News and Notes." November 15, 1881.

Port Jervis Evening Gazette. "Brief Mention." November 1, 1870.

———. "The Brooks Case." July 19, 1909.

———. "Death of John Babbitt." July 6, 1913.

———. "Ghost of Emma Brooks Appears." Sept 14, 1909.

———. "Has a Bad Record." March 17, 1913.

———. "Insane Patient Takes His Life." November 14, 1913.

———. "A Mute Murderer on Trial." October 11, 1870.

Portsmouth Herald, "Grand Jury Reports Forty Seven Indictments." April 17, 1913.

———. "John Babbitt Claims to Have Murdered Emma Brooks in Ulster Co., New York 4 Years Ago." March 10, 1913.

———. "New York Officer Here Hears Details of Confession from Babbitt and Is Convinced That He Murdered Emma Brooks." March 17, 1913

———. "New York Officials Are Anxious about Babbitt's Condition." March 13, 1913.

———. "Prisoners at the Hospital Show Signs of Recovery." March 11,1913.

———. "Their Liberty Was of Short Duration." June 3, 1913.

Rockland County Times. "A House Is a House: Clergyman's Hut Knocks Out Hotel Keeper's Plans." December 13, 1902.

Syracuse New York Daily Journal. "Three Dying of Knife Wounds." November 26, 1907.

Troy Daily Times. "Legally Hanged, Louis Willett, the Murderer of Edwin Kelland, Hanged at Kingston." May 21, 1886.

ABOUT THE AUTHORS

A.J. Schenkman is a social studies teacher in Ulster County and a freelance writer. He is the author of the popular *Wicked Ulster County: Tales of Desperadoes, Gangs and More* (The History Press) as well as two earlier publications, *Washington's Headquarters in Newburgh* (Arcadia Publishing) and *Washington's Headquarters: Home to a Revolution* (The History Press). He has published numerous articles on Hudson Valley history in publications such as

A.J. Schenkman's collection.

Ulster Magazine, the *Times Herald-Record, Chronogram* and on his website, Ulster County History Journal (www.ucnyistory.com). Mr. Schenkman also serves on the Friends of Senate House Board of Trustees in Kingston, New York.

Elizabeth Werlau is an English teacher in New York State's Hudson Valley region. She is the author of *Images of America: Plattekill* and *Hallowed Grounds: Historic Cemeteries of the Town of Plattekill, NY* (coauthored with Shirley Anson). In addition, she has published numerous articles on the Hudson Valley for the *Times* community newspapers of the Hudson Valley, *Hudson Valley Business Journal* and on her website, Ulster County History Journal (www.ucnyhistory.com). Ms. Werlau currently serves as president of the Plattekill Historical Society, as a member of the board of directors of the Ulster County Historical Society and as a researcher/writer for the Wallkill Valley Land Trust's annual Houses on the Land tours.